Angela Blakey

WHEN THE CORN IS RIPE

A Christian's Way of
Learning to Die

VERITAS

First published 1993 by
Veritas Publications
7-8 Lower Abbey Street
Dublin 1

ISBN 1 85390 260 8

**British Library Cataloguing
in Publication Data.**
A catalogue record for
this book is available
from the British Library.

Cover design by creative a.d., Dublin
Cover illustration reproduced with permission of
The Slide File, Dublin
Printed in the Republic of Ireland by
The Criterion Press Ltd, Dublin

CONTENTS

Part I

Part II

Part III

Part IV

Part V

Part VI

Acknowledgement

I give my very grateful thanks to my husband, Redvers, for his living inspiration and his patient correction of my inaccurate manuscripts; to my daughter, Clare, for her unwavering support; to Sr Jean Kirkpatrick and Rev. John Wilcox for their timely encouragement, and to Linda McGrath and the many other bereaved people whose pain I have been privileged to share.

All royalties on the sales of this book will go to Teesside Hospice Care Foundation.

INTRODUCTION

'How morbid to be so concerned about death!' said a friend, shuddering.

In case she was right, I checked on the meaning of morbid – 'abnormal; diseased; gloomy; gruesome; pathological' (*Penguin English Dictionary*).

But we have to admit that there's nothing so universally 'normal' as dying, is there? And does death *have* to be either 'gloomy' or 'gruesome'? Maybe if we weren't so obsessed with staying alive, we could come to see death as the climax of our lives?

Freud put it even more bluntly when he said that death is the *aim* of life.

There must be a high proportion of medical resources being concentrated on trying to avoid that aim! Rather than clinging to life at all costs, could we learn to prepare for death with at least as much thoroughness as we would prepare for any other great event in our lives? We wouldn't change jobs without a great deal of consideration. We wouldn't emigrate without a lot of research. Nor would we drift thoughtlessly into marriage. Even an annual holiday is well prepared for.

In contrast to this, most of us seem to approach death looking the other way! Like Woody Allen, I don't mind about dying – I just don't want to be around when it happens!

We wouldn't cross the road as carelessly as some of us go towards the greatest experience of our lives – meeting our Creator!

I'm sure we've got death all wrong. Blame society, our culture, the Church, the state or who you will – but where do we turn to get it right?

I certainly can't claim any expertise! I, who at the sight of a coffin or a freshly dug grave, become emotionally incontinent! All I can offer is a share in my struggle to learn.

There can be only one teacher – the one who made us and designed death as an integral part of our lives.

God has an overall plan for the whole of humankind, in which we are slender but necessary threads. To God, there was purpose in the timing of our birth. There is equal significance in the hour of our death. Neither our birth nor our death is a punishment. Birth and death are our opportunities to become co-creators with God.

This loving God, who knew us before we were born – who wastes nothing, not even our mistakes – will never let us slip out of his knowing. He will meet us and know us at our death, as we too will know him.

So why do we shy away from this encounter? Why do we build such an emotional barricade around that moment? Perhaps because we don't really know the one we go to meet! Maybe if we could put that right to some extent, death would not be so terrifying. We could face it at least with equanimity, and possibly even excitement!

1

TODAY WE HAVE THE GIFT OF LIFE

If today I discovered that I was terminally ill, what chaos would churn through my mind. What a lot I would need to put right – besides trying to sort out the shoe cupboard!

The more I consider the imaginary catalogue, the more it makes sense to do something about things today. Why delay? I might not get the timing right!

Relationships would have to top my list – all the misunderstanding, meanness and self-centredness that over the years have skewed friendships. All the neglects, and the kind things I *meant* to do. (Come to think of it, Lord, I need a good few years of grace, even starting today!)

But besides rectifying past problems, *now* is the time to celebrate life to the full. Every day is a fresh start, a new experience. Every moment of each day, every breath we take, is pure gift from God, given with unconditional love.

'No one has anything unless God gives it to him' (John 3:27). The least we can do is accept it, enjoy it, and respond as best we can to that love.

How strangely difficult that can be at times! The clue must surely be in being like a child. Children happily survive any turmoil so long as they know that they are well loved.

We are incredibly well loved. Jesus insists that God the Father loves us equally with himself (John 17:23).

It's easy to believe that the Father loves the Son, because he is worthy of that love. But me? Can I possibly be loved like that? Without doing anything to deserve it?

As Christians, we must come to believe – YES! 'We too are his children' (Acts 17:28). 'And since you are his children, God will give you all that he has' (Galatians 4:7). That's an awe-full lot of love!

Outrageous as it may seem, God loves us *all*. Not just

those who are good, or handsome, or clever, or responsive, but *all* of us. Isn't that cause enough to celebrate daily? Why are we so subdued about it?

Maybe we haven't the capacity to receive all God's love in this life on earth, but we can certainly begin to accept as much as possible, and gradually increase our capacity.

So how do we start celebrating our being alive?

Getting to know Christ

'Christ is the visible likeness of the invisible God' (Colossians 1:15). 'He reflects the brightness of God's glory and is the exact likeness of God's own being' (Hebrews 1:3).

If I had a distant cousin coming from America, naturally I would try to find out all that I could about her and her interests. There would be plans made to do things together. Then I'd spring-clean, paint up the shabby bits and set off with curiosity to meet her.

Surely the process of getting to know the Lord is somewhat similar?

Firstly, we find out all we can about him from his friends – writers, speakers, thinkers, priests and teachers; and then from his biography – the New Testament. Here, every word can be searched and felt and responded to, in an attempt to explore the character and thinking of this man, Jesus Christ. This is our resource book, the study of which is liable to turn into a love affair.

Cool research gradually develops into a personal and intimate relationship with Jesus Christ – an extremely provocative, controversial and fascinating man, who is forever inviting us into a very close partnership. '... come to me in order to have life' (John 5:40). 'Remain united to me, and I will remain united to you'(John 15:4). 'Come to me, all of you who are tired from carrying heavy loads, and I will give you rest' (Matthew 11:28).

Secondly, we deliberately plan to spend time with this

man, discovering activities that we can do with him, in him and through him. This way, we will have a relationship that is unique – faulty and limited as it is on our part, but faithful and enhancing on his.

This is a lifetime's work, and panic can rise in me again because I haven't started early enough! But Jesus is a marvellous teacher, one to one, at my pace, and very patient with a late developer. We do however, need to be keen to learn.

When Jesus lived on earth, ordinary people walked miles and miles to meet him, and they clamoured to hear his every word. 'He began to teach them many things' (Mark 6:34), and when I make the effort to meet him and listen, this is my experience too.

He *chooses* to be with ordinary people, in our ordinary lives, and he teaches through the simple, everyday events. Indeed, he can transform our very ordinariness. Life in his company is good. That's part of the love affair. 'He is the key that opens all the hidden treasures of God's wisdom and knowledge' (Colossians 2:3).

This is the Man whom we believe to be God's Messiah – the Anointed One, the Son of God, 'the light that comes into the world and shines on everyone' (John 1:9). It is belief in him that makes us Christians. 'Believe in the light ... so that you will be the people of the light' (John 12:36).

This is the man who invites us to partner him! Who puts us equal in value to his mother and brothers, if only we will believe in him and obey his teachings. That is the potential of our relationship. 'How happy are those who have no doubts about me!' (Matthew 11:6).

Jesus urges us into an incredibly close union with himself so that 'in him we live and move and exist' (Acts 17:28). If we join ourselves to the Lord, we become spiritually one with him – we ordinary people! We would be on a permanent high if we really realised and accepted!

Gradually we come to understand that we accomplish

11

nothing worthwhile outside our life in Christ. This can mean that we look back over our past lives and see that we have accomplished very little! If at death we are to be pruned of all that has not come from God, how much will be left of our personalities, our achievements, our relationships, our everything?

While on earth, he desired such close unity with his disciples that he offered them his own Body and Blood. 'Whoever eats my flesh and drinks my blood lives in me, and I live in him' (John 6:56). Many of his followers left him at this point, as many reject the Eucharist today, but he said: 'I am the living bread that comes down from heaven. If anyone eats this bread, he will live for ever' (John 6:51).

This is Jesus offering us the food of eternal life, not only for life after death, but also to enrich our present lives on earth. He said: 'I have come in order that you might have life – life in all its fullness' (John 10:10) – right *now*.

Christ is to be the focus of our lives. Then Christ will be our focus as we die. It is Christ whom we will meet at the point of our death. It is Christ who has redeemed us.

He leads us to God the Father: '... whoever accepts the Son has the Father also' (1 John 2:23). We don't have to wait for the next world to begin to know our Father. Through Christ we begin to know him here. We will not meet as strangers when we die.

Throughout Christ's public life, he frequently drew away from the crowds to be alone with his Father. If *he* needed to, we certainly do too. To learn to be alone with the Father, listening and attentive, would be the best skill we could acquire before we come to die. But even if we have never found a lonely place to be with him, we can be sure that he will find us in the loneliness of dying. Dare we risk this being the first time that we are alone together?

Mind you, I can well imagine that some souls who meet Christ as a stranger at the point of death, will have an overwhelming experience of love at first sight, without any of the hang-ups of church introductions! However, we can't presume, and if *now* is the time when Christ makes himself known, *now* is the appropriate time to respond. He may have work for us, today, in this place.

How can we respond to his love?
'God loves you and has chosen you to be his own' (1 Thessalonians 1:4).

To know we are so intensely and unconditionally loved calls for daily celebration.

Jesus seems to have enjoyed celebrating. He was at a wedding feast when he performed his first miracle. Here, at Cana, this miracle of water into the finest wine was both fun and extravagant. (You should see the size of the water pots!)

Jesus didn't choose to emerge into the public eye during a serious or pompous occasion, but at a party! There, in the middle of laughing and chattering with his friends, 'He revealed his glory, and his disciples believed in him' (John 2:11).

We too must believe in him, and imitation is the best way we can celebrate God's love in our own lives: 'Since you are God's dear children, you must try to be like him' (Ephesians 5:1).

He wants our hearts, like his, to be full of active love. Indeed, he's not really interested in too much else. Had we his vision, every individual would be equally valued and treasured. Each encounter would be further cause for celebration.

Our God is not heavy with sadness, nor spiked with anger as some church services would have us suspect. He is the light – our light – and part of our celebration is to reflect that light, even in adversity. Even in the very serious adversity of terminal illness.

Belief, light, love and celebration are distinctly active rather than passive. Therefore, long before approaching death drains us of our vigour, we have a need to serve God's people with energy. This we do for God's glory, not our own. Oh, what tricky motivation there can be within this striving to love!

'... he who wants glory* for the one who sent him is honest, and there is nothing false in him' (John 7:18). (Lord, please bless us with such honesty!)

In response to his love, we are drawn to listen to him and so to come to obey him. Look and listen: 'I give you a new commandment: love one another' (John 13:34). COMMAND! Not a request or advice, but a direct order, and unless we consciously try to obey that order, we do not follow Christ. We are not Christians.

But there are two parts to this order, if we listen carefully – 'Love *one another*', he said, and that implies both giving and receiving love. Some of us can love so aggressively that we forget to submit ourselves to being loved by others.

Learning to love and be loved is the whole curriculum of the Christian school of life – an intricate and delicate art to acquire. Do Christian schools give this subject priority over all others? If they don't or can't, then they are pointless institutions – as are all other nominally Christian communities.

Mind, heart, spirit and body are all meant to participate in this learning to love. Wholeness results if we can get it right. Distortions occur if one part is over-emphasised or another neglected. Hardness and bitterness develop if love is meagre. We are handicapped personalities if we are not loved enough or can't accept the love on offer. There can be pitfalls, pains, obstacles and rejection; also joys, peace, vision and light, and Jesus Christ knows all these facets of love.

'As I have loved you, so you must love one another' (John 13:34). That means being actively compassionate, forgiving, accepting and delighting in his people. It is being both

---

* See the definition of GLORY: splendour; heavenly bliss; triumphant honour; beauty; resplendent brightness; summit of attainment or gratification; a burst of sunlight; the presence of God; a representation of the heavens opened; to rejoice. (*Chambers Twentieth Century Dictionary*)

available and vulnerable. '... it is not by hearing the Law that people are put right with God, but by *doing* what the Law commands' (Romans 2:13).

But we can't do all this loving on our own. We have to team up with the Father and use his strength, discernment and sensitivity – as Jesus did. Then honour and glory goes to the one who gave us all in the first place.

And look: '... in all things God works for good with those who love him' (Romans 8:28). *All things* – that includes the trivia and the troubles, and our dying.

Love is our passport to heaven. Our entrance fee. Our currency. *Now* is our opportunity to build up our treasury.

Accept from God all the love we can and invest it in everyone else. This is one way in which God's love becomes experienced within our secular world. These are the 'talents' that he wants us to put to good use.

Our love of God must always take priority above our love of anyone else. Anything other than this is idolatry. 'Whoever comes to me cannot be my disciple unless he loves me more than he loves his father and his mother, his wife and his children, his brothers and his sisters, and himself as well' (Luke 14:26).

God is the one who gifts us with all these people and obviously the giver is to be honoured more than the gifts he gives .

God's love is so extravagant that it can seem impossible to respond to it adequately, and of course, it is. But God is pleased out of all proportion with what we do. Every small gift of love is valued by him.

Mary broke open a jar of very expensive perfume and emptied the contents over Jesus. He said 'It is a fine and beautiful thing that she has done for me ...' (Matthew 26:10).

It is my belief that we will all get the opportunity to do a fine and beautiful thing for him. Possibly it will be the willing gift of ourselves or our loved ones in death. Maybe this is to be our ultimate response to his love.

Living according to his plan

'... he sits down first and works out what it will cost' (Luke 14:28).

This working out can only be done alone with God, chewing things over, allowing the Holy Spirit a large input. Then, hopefully, we will come to discernment – always a tricky problem for me. How much is my initiative, how much the Holy Spirit's?

Time for prayer is essential if we are to learn to live according to his plan. Although God is always with us, and a word of thanks or praise can constantly punctuate our work and play, no relationship develops on asides only. An intensity of stillness and togetherness is always important for a deepening friendship.

There are so many forms of prayer and so many ways of praying that can't be explored here. However, in working out the cost, we must take into account both the time to be alone with God and the time to come together before God.

Apart from any other consideration, around the experience of death there is a great need for prayer. How much easier that will be if it is already a well-established skill.

My own experience has been that the quality of prayer very slowly improves with practice, and God gradually gives us a heightened awareness of his constant presence. A life of prayer would fill both life and death with hope and joy.

But '... faith without actions is dead' (James 2:26). 'God ... has created us for a life of good deeds, which he has already prepared for us to do' (Ephesians 2:10). It is important, then, that we do *those* deeds, and don't go dashing off to do what we *imagine* to be good deeds. We are to be responsive to his will, always.

'All things are done according to God's plan and decision; and God chose us to be his own people in union with Christ because of his own purpose, based on what he had decided from the very beginning' (Ephesians 1:11).

Do we know what God's purpose has been for us so far?

Have we attempted to find out?

Have we known full well, and resisted it?

Or is our sin more of indifference? What a sin that is, considering the circumstances!

We are such ignorant creatures for God to have given the dangerous gift of free will to! Our only rightful role is that of servant to the Almighty, and we are exceedingly privileged to be that.

True love of God would draw us voluntarily to become his servants – at his beck and call, available to please his every whim – including answering his call to join him in his Kingdom! 'Whoever wants to serve me must follow me, so that my servant will be with me where I am' (John 12:26).

Where, then, is Jesus? For certain he is with the poor, the suffering, the rejected, the oppressed, the imprisoned, the inadequate, the dying and the bereaved.

Where are we? Are we obedient to the will of the Father who sent Jesus to these people in 30AD and is sending us to them in the twentieth century?

'God in his grace chose me even before I was born, and called me to serve him' (Galatians 1:15). But to be a servant is not a twentieth century aim. It is so foreign to my previous ambitions that I have difficulty defining the qualities of a good servant! The list on the next page may help in this.

17

Servanthood	Christ, the Master we Serve
1. Obedient	'Do whatever he tells you' (John 2:5).
2. Well-trained	Read 2 Peter 1:3,5-8
3. Disciplined	'Every athlete in training submits to strict discipline' (l Corinthians 9:25).
4. Hard-working	'Keep busy always in your work for the Lord, since you know that nothing you do in the Lord's service is ever useless' (l Corinthians 15:58).
5. Anticipate my master's desires	'...try to find out what the Lord wants you to do' (Ephesians 5:17).
6. Want to please	'Happy are those whose greatest desire is to do what God requires' (Matthew 5:6).
7. Faithful	'....stand firm in your life in the Lord' (Philippians 4:1).
8. Take pride in my master	'....whatever you do .... do it all for God's glory' (l Corinthians 10:31).
9. Contented in service	'I have learnt to be satisfied with what I have' (Philippians 4:11).
10. Subordinate	'....I do nothing on my own authority, but I say only what the Father has instructed me to say' (John 8:28).

Jesus was subordinate to the authority of his Father – he, who is God's son. How often we strut about, flaunting our own authority rather than God's!

It seems to me that the world is in its adolescent stage of spiritual development – we are no longer mindlessly and slavishly obedient to the law. Personal freedom obsesses us now, at the expense of everything else. I suspect that to become mature Christians, we will have to get round to relinquishing that freedom voluntarily in order to serve God.

'I always do what pleases him' (John 8:29), said Jesus – the perfect servant.

I am still an appalling servant. A lesser master would have sacked me long ago! But if we allow him, God will eventually fashion us into the mould of a good servant in order to build up the Body of Christ. This is God's purpose for us. We are not in the business of feathering our own spiritual nests, but in that of preparing to be sent out to serve others with love and joy.

As servants of God, we have to strive for incredibly high standards. 'You must be perfect – just as your Father in heaven is perfect!' (Matthew 5:48). Christ won't have asked the impossible of us. This is our true potential and God could make it possible, but we put up tremendous blocks to such overwhelming grace. We deem ourselves not worthy – and we are not – but then our worthiness is not the criterion of God's mercy and grace.

We need to become as full of grace as we possibly can, in order to do God's work well. Especially the work of sharing our knowledge of Christ and his divine message to all humankind.

The members of the early Church prayed. '... allow us, your servants, to speak your message with all boldness... through the name of your holy Servant Jesus' (Acts 4:29-30). That surely has to be part of God's plan for all of us – that we speak of God's love for us and his promise of eternal life.

19

If we fail to do this, we might be denying others their opportunity to share in God's creative work of building his Kingdom. How dare we risk that?

The gift of God's Word is not given to us in secret to be hidden from the rest. The Word we have received is to be put to use like yeast or like incense: 'God uses us to make the knowledge about Christ spread everywhere like a sweet fragrance' (2 Corinthians 2:14).

Do we share the Word with our friends today? Yet why else have we been born? Been baptised? Why else have we been given the Word?

Can we speak of his love and his promise through the way that we approach our death? Lord, I have the awful feeling that for years I've missed the whole point of life! I've hardly started on the job of getting to know you, responding to your love, discerning your plan, becoming your servant and sharing your teachings.

Before it is too late I want to begin to work for the accolade of 'faithful servant', and I can draw comfort from the fact that however poor I am now, you will put even my blatant failures to good use.

May your Holy Spirit bring order out of the chaos within me.]

Accepting God's Holy Spirit

'God has poured out his love into our hearts by means of the Holy Spirit, who is God's gift to us all' (Romans 5:5).

We are given the impression of the Spirit being an avalanche of Godness pouring into us. We can try to stand rock-hard against it. We can try to hide from its force. Or we can soak it up like a sponge. The more sodden we become, the more we can drench others. 'Whoever believes in me, streams of life-giving water will pour out from his heart' (John 7:38).

Do we want to be sponges or rocks?

Are we afraid of the need to change?

'Do not be afraid', the Bible tells us – 365 times I'm told, though I haven't checked it. But '... the Spirit that God has given us does not make us timid; instead, his Spirit fills us with power, love, and self-control' (2 Timothy 1:7).

God's Spirit – given to us in Baptism and on tap thereafter – has already given us all that we need both to live and to die for him. If we accept his Spirit and use all the gifts the Spirit offers us, then we automatically build up and strengthen the whole people of God. Our gifts will be specific to the job in hand, including facing death.

We cannot choose our gifts, nor should we be disgruntled with them. What we have is what we need and we must be careful not to set our hearts on a more glamorous job than we are given.

To recognise, acknowledge and accept our gifts will guide us towards our appointed work. Others will affirm and encourage our choice if it is right. There is a strange passivity in learning to absorb God's Holy Spirit, as if we have to learn to relax.

We cannot demand the Spirit as of right. It is simply poured into us when we stop blocking it. When we stop striving to succeed on our own, we discover that the Spirit empowers us.

If we resist the Spirit, we cannot know God, we cannot pray. We can neither hear nor interpret God's message.

If we accept the Spirit we will experience God in all that is good. We will be allowed to share in his creating. We will know peace and joy even in the chaos of this world. We will enjoy all the happiness that the Lord blesses us with. Such happiness may not last for ever. There is no reason why it should. That's all the more reason for enjoying it while we can and for praising and thanking God for it.

To accept the Spirit is to hear and act upon God's message. It is to have moments of transfiguration, when we will touch the wonder of God.

21

God's Spirit gives value to all that we do, and enables us to have a growing, living relationship with God. The Spirit is that relationship, and can be in all our relationships.

Those who are Spirit-filled are full of life and they will not lose that life at death. Indeed, our capacity to accept the Spirit will then be so great that God's avalanche of love will totally envelop us. Happy the hour of our death!

The Spirit is free and unrestrainable. Those who try to contain the power of the Spirit are doomed to failure. People who proclaim that someone will not get to heaven for this or that reason, are attempting to tie the Spirit to some law. But God's Holy Spirit is greater than any law. 'Do not restrain the Holy Spirit' (1 Thessalonians 5:19). '... where the Spirit of the Lord is present, there is freedom' (2 Corinthians 3:17).

So our long-term preparation for our personal resurrection is to become fully open to the Holy Spirit in this life. 'If the Spirit of God ... lives in you, then he who raised Christ from death will also give life to your mortal bodies by the presence of his Spirit in you' (Romans 8:11).

Just think – were we to accept God's Holy Spirit, we have the means to bring about God's will, here on earth as it is in heaven. What is there to do *now* that is more important than taking time out to open ourselves to that Spirit? 'This is the hour to receive God's favour' (2 Corinthians 6:2).

Accepting God's promise of eternal life
'Whoever believes in the Son has eternal life' (John 3:36).

'My sheep listen to my voice; I know them, and they follow me. I give them eternal life, and they shall never die. No one can snatch them away from me' (John 10:27-28).

If we are real followers of Christ, then we live our lives according to that promise of eternal life. Our whole lives will be focused on that future.

Like a good driver, looking to the end of the road and constantly adjusting the position of the car in order to get there safely, our eyes are to be fixed on eternal life and adjustments made to our lifestyle in order to arrive there safely.

Decisions will be made in the light of that future, paths will be chosen that lead to that destination. It is neither too early nor too late to search for those paths and set off along them. We need the paths to be so familiar that we could follow them blindfolded – or with any other handicap we might develop! At the end of the path, we will meet Christ. That meeting is our promised delight, and God's purpose in creating us.

It stands to reason that when God has loved us so much on earth, he will not discard us at death. All the love that has been invested in us, and all the love we have passed on, will survive with us into that promised future.

Maybe, in some small way, we are even allowed to influence some aspect of everlasting life. Do we cooperate with God in the creation of heaven then? My God, we are so slow to catch on!

Do we fear death because we have missed the whole point of life?

[Lord, help us to grasp and hang on to the truth of your divine love and mercy. Fill us with your holy Spirit, so that we will come to love and serve you more and more, every day of our lives. Make us realise that you want us to live with the joyful certainty of eternal life, and to share our conviction with others. Lord, in your mercy, hear our cry.]

2

PRACTICE DEATHS

We cannot get through life without a series of loss experiences. These are amongst the many ways we are forced to practise death. How we cope with these inevitable losses will very probably indicate how we will tackle our own death.

In looking that supposition in the face, I'm brought to realise how much practice I need, as many losses leave me angry and resentful, and that isn't how I want to die.

So is dying a skill that can be learnt, like skiing? We are useless and maybe frightened to begin with, but after lots of practice of the simple techniques on the nursery slopes, we gain skill and confidence until we are ready to face the ultimate challenge – alone, off piste!

This is surely exciting! Exhilarating! Worth all the practice! And the earlier one starts learning, the better!

To me, the basic skill of learning to die would seem to be learning to let go. Letting go of possessions; of people; of self. '... none of you can be my disciple unless he gives up everything he has' (Luke 14:33).

A hard gospel to follow, but we can come to it gradually by training ourselves in a thousand small ways. And we never work alone. Even very small gestures of letting go can be our starting-point – not having a biscuit or another cup of coffee; putting down the paper to listen to someone who wants to talk; turning the telly off sometimes so that we can be more sensitive to the real world.

These are mere crumbs to offer to God, but far from sneering, he has the knack of converting crumbs into cake. Maybe we will never have more than crumbs to offer God before our death, but: 'Whoever is faithful in small matters will be faithful in large ones' (Luke 16:10). It is the relinquishing of our hold on anything *for God's sake* that gives value to the smallest act.

Letting go of possessions

For anyone else like me, who is starting from scratch, there would appear to be a logical order to learning this skill:

First: Clear out the junk, preferably for recycling. The memorabilia drawer can be checked as we ask ourselves why we are keeping this or that. Are we excessively focused on the past? Or are we hoping our descendants will discover some jewel of our nature that we have modestly kept hidden from them in our lifetime? The 'might-come-in-useful-one-day' cupboard can probably be emptied wholesale into the bin or jumble sale, along with spare pairs and spare parts.

Second: The things of value that we don't much treasure can be sold and the money given to the poor. The charity shops do that job brilliantly for us.

Third: Giving away what we would really like to keep – and here the skills practice grows a little harder, but believe what Jesus said: 'There is more happiness in giving than in receiving'(Acts 20:35). We can start with giving to those we love, then graduate to giving to those we love less, and better still – to give in secret to those in need. This gets easier in later life. The struggle to provide adequately for one's immediate family is over and we can begin to focus on the wider family of God. Unfortunately, it's also the time of life when we are tempted to amass the beautiful. But no real Christian should be an avid collector. Christ collected nothing. And when one's home stands elegantly simple and unadorned – think how easy the dusting will be! And think how pleasant it will be to travel light! The gathering of trivia and riches puts millstones around the neck. I grow light-hearted at the prospect, but need as yet to put the theory into practice.

Fourth: Those who are creative craftworkers have the opportunity to give away what they create. It is all too easy to hug to oneself the more successful efforts, like holding on to a favourite child, but 'God loves the one who gives gladly' (2 Corinthians 9:7).

Fifth: Then there is the lure of getting rich. How we are warned to resist: 'Do not store riches up for yourselves here on earth ... for your heart will always be where your riches are' (Matthew 6:19,21).

'It is much harder for a rich person to enter the kingdom of God than for a camel to go through the eye of a needle' (Mark 10:25).

Words to make all those with a healthy bank balance tremble, until Jesus throws a lifeline: 'This is impossible for man but for God everything is possible'. This surely makes us all – rich and poor alike – realise our total dependence upon God. Even the *good* rich man of the Gospels couldn't get to heaven under his own steam. How is it, that for us acquisitive mortals, the incredible riches of heaven fail to outweigh the attraction of trivial riches here on earth? Are we not prepared to wait? Do we doubt? Lack imagination? Or is it pure greed? Some of us have to do a lot of learning to let go! Hopefully, one day, we will all come to be able to say, with Paul, 'For his sake I have thrown everything away; I consider it all as mere refuse, so that I may gain Christ and be completely united with him' (Philippians 3:8-9).

Letting go of people

And here I haven't even got a method to suggest! The more we love, the more pain there is in letting go, but practise it we must, starting from parting with our children to school, to college, to work, and on to the fiercely difficult thing of parting from our treasured partner.

But we own no one. All belong to God, and each must be allowed to find their own way to grow towards him. His plan is different for each one of us. We have neither the right nor the ability to choose another's path.

Then, others have repeatedly to let go of us, and being let go of can sometimes be as scary as the letting go.

Married couples, close as they are intended to be, have

also got to learn how to give each other space to be fulfilled. It's all too easy to suffocate one another.

This constant untying process is hard to learn for those of us with strong tendencies to cling. Even moving house can be a disturbing loss of relationships and roots. But we are to be '... as strangers and refugees in this world!' (1 Peter 2:11), a sense we lose if we are too securely rooted in bricks and mortar. The rich are in danger again – they have had their security!

Letting go of self
The hardest letting go of all, perhaps. There are parallels to the skills of letting go of possessions:

1. Start with throwing out the junk! For example – practise dumping unnecessary loads. These may be part of our self-importance rather than Christ's work.

2. Let go of the strong competitive instincts that are so carefully nurtured by our education system. Find out that we can take great pleasure in another's success.

3. Let go of pretence. We are all vulnerable, mistaken and incomplete. Why do we try so hard to disguise this fact from one another? We are human. We are not God. We are fallible.

If we stop pretending, stop masking our deficiencies, we can come to the point of accepting our limitations, faults, inadequacies and ridiculousness, so acknowledging our frailty and mortality, our fears and doubts and our need of each other, coming eventually to the knowledge that God loves us through all this.

4. To accept our infinitesimal smallness; to accept our comicness; to reject the temptation to glorify ourselves, and come to rejoice in the growth, achievements and status of others – all this is learning to die to self. Then, through our failures, thwarted plans and rejections – we can come to see God's plan within adversity. I suspect that failure forms the very soil of heaven, or maybe it is more like the smelly compost!

Learning to let go this way will make us more real to others, as we shed protective layers. And perhaps God only wants to look on our reality and smile!

5. Let go of our sins and open ourselves to change – as we have explored earlier.

6. Let go of our harboured revenges. We are to forgive 490 times, as God in his mercy has already done for us. It would pay us to become outrageously merciful, and he will do the same. To forgive is to practise dying to self.

7. Let go of our love of constant noise and company, sometimes choosing, as Jesus did, a silent place to listen to the Father.

8. Move over, letting others in, be it on a crowded bus, or moving off a committee where we have enjoyed serving for far too long!

9. Fasting – a relinquishing of one's innocent desires. So closely linked with Christ at prayer.

10. Keep quiet, not interfering, in spite of longing to share our obviously greater wisdom!

11. We can deflect the acclaim that may come our way for some apparent achievement, and in our hearts, attribute the success where it belongs – to God himself.

12. Could we cultivate a willingness to let go of the secure? To take risks in response to his will? From knocking on a stranger's door to share Christ's message, to any adventurous journey that he chooses to lead us into. And death must be the greatest adventure of them all.

So we are learning to say 'Yes' to God when we're not particularly keen. Becoming obedient to his will. We are learning to let go of earthly props and cling only to the Lord, as Peter did when floundering in the water. Or, better still, learning to walk on water, knowing God holds us up.

To allow ourselves to drop off the stalk, like a grain of wheat, into the unexplored depths of God's love – with total trust in him – that is learning to die to self. Any prayer where we choose to release ourselves into God's care is practice death, and turns us into his listening and obedient servants.

'If you hear God's voice today, do not be stubborn' (Hebrews 3:15). Stubborn – a real clinging on to set opinions and set ways.

'... the kind of man I like', says the Lord, 'is a man who will do all I want him to do.' Which may not be much! And may not be what I want to do! But through it all, we are acquiring poverty of spirit, and that is surely the right gear for our practice sessions!

The ageing process enforces much letting go – of looks, abilities and opportunities, but most of all, of health and strength. We can kick and scream and sulk in protest at these losses, or we can put all in God's hands. As our youth and vitality are God-given, so too has he designed the process of decline. It must have its purpose and I must struggle to welcome both with equal enthusiasm. God help me!

'Whoever makes himself great will be humbled, and whoever humbles himself will be made great' (Matthew 23:12). And when we are sick, we can indeed be humbled in many ways. To submit cheerfully to the inevitable letting go of one's dignity has the promise of great things through Christ, who humbled himself far beyond our apprehension.

Christ's *kenosis* – his supreme letting go of both his Godliness and his humanity, first at his Incarnation, then at his Crucifixion. He gave up all, in spite of having supreme power. There is no limit to what Jesus could have done to avert this 'failure', but he *chose* not to. Will we ever appreciate what Christ did for us?

Maybe only he can empty himself totally, but we can choose to submit to being emptied all the way along the line until the final letting go in death – the complete surrender to the will of God.

'Our Lord Jesus Christ, rich as he was, he made himself poor for your sake, in order to make you rich by means of his poverty' (2 Corinthians 8:9). Maybe, in some small way, we too have the means of making others slightly richer by our becoming poorer. We do nothing in isolation for ourselves alone. Nor does God waste the merest crumb of love.

'If you are eager to give, God will accept your gift on the basis of what you have to give, not on what you haven't' (2 Corinthians 8:12).

Jesus said to his Father 'All I have is yours' (John 17:10). If he can say that, how much more appropriate a prayer it is for us. *Nothing* is ours to keep. All is God's. The sooner we get that perspective on life, the better we'll be prepared for death, as 'nothing' is very easy to leave behind.

But Jesus goes on to say to the Father '... and all you have is mine' (John 17:10). This too will be true for us in our eternal life. But the exchange can begin here on earth, as we learn to surrender more and more to God. He won't be ungenerous in the rate of exchange! He is helping us throughout our spiritual growth, as we attempt to alter the focus from self to him. As our skills develop, he will grow greater while we become smaller – the very essence of learning to die.

Eventually, God-guided, we must believe that we will come to the point where we choose to contemplate God rather than ourselves; where we abandon our own expectations in favour of God's plan; and we come to live a life fully controlled by his will, not our desires.

So we shall find that our practice deaths carry us closer to our final death, but 'Even though our physical being is gradually decaying, yet our spiritual being is renewed day after day' (2 Corinthians 4:16).

And one brilliant test of whether we are getting our act together is – are we full of joy? Because joy and a deep peace are the outward sign of the Spirit at work within us.

'My heart is ready, O God, my heart is ready' (Psalm 56:8), at least to *start* work on this daily practice, and what better prayer is there to finish on?

3

CONTEMPLATING OUR OWN DEATH

'Make us know the shortness of our life
that we may gain wisdom of heart' (Psalm 89:12).

It pays us to get used to the idea that we are going to die, rather than collaborate with our death-denying society.

The Old Testament contains a delightful phrase: 'a tender affection for life'! And isn't that what most of us have while we are blessed with health and strength of mind and body?

The fact is that old age diminishes this health and strength, as can accident and illness at any age. Even then, the will to live often remains very powerful, sometimes beyond reason or wisdom.

I don't want to be like that. I want to learn how to accept all that God throws to me in life, and all he offers me when dying, with at least equal fascination.

God, please help me to do this.

I suppose all of life is the opportunity to orientate oneself to death, anticipating re-birth; re-creation; re-formation; re-union; re-newal. This is something which will happen to *all* the people of God. How best can we whole-heartedly cooperate with God in this re-orientation?

How do we stand full square and face the certainty of death and still enjoy the fullness of life right up to the end? Some people do! Surely, part of the art of dying must be to have entered thoroughly into living without losing sight of the ultimate experience?

'Throughout our lives we are always in danger of death ... death is at work in us' (2 Corinthians 4:11-12). As soon as we are born, we are on our journey towards death. No one can reverse the process or change the direction. But also from birth, we are moving towards his Kingdom and his Glory.

31

Heaven can hold no fears. It is simply a change of place. A drastic change, but distinctly for the better. Anticipation, awe, excitement, fascination, expectation, are all more reasonable emotions than fear. A Christian's death should be different – it is the final journey of a believer returning to God. Our Creator will not abandon his children on that journey. We have nothing to fear.

So death itself is not fearful, but the *how* of dying can contain fears.

Will we die of old age – gradually losing faculties, freedom and personality?

Will death sneak up on us unexpectedly, or is everyone subconsciously warned?

Will we be able to concentrate on God, or will pain, pills and confusion muddle us?

Could we be in God's company within the silent stillness of a stroke?

Surely God prepares his children for their greatest adventure? Or are we meant to have done an ongoing preparation throughout our lives? Preparing our wedding garment for the feast?

Jesus said to Matthew 'Come', and he got up, leaving everything and went with Jesus. Will we be bidden so abruptly?

'"Come, everything is ready!" But they all began, one after another, to make excuses' (Luke 14:17). Do we do this as death approaches? 'Not yet Lord!' These pills; this operation; this replacement. For the young – yes. The middle-aged – maybe. But the elderly? Doesn't age teach us wisdom and acceptance of the will of God? Having said that, it is often the relatives of the elderly who won't let go!

Will we meet some tragic end before we have time to argue – smashed in a car, a plane, or a train? Caught in a volcano, a hurricane or tidal wave? Or be the victim of some horrific, human violence?

Will this involve great pain; great fear? The worst situations bring out the very best in some people, but the trouble is, we can't know how we might react. We could be shattered by our own lack of heroism!

If we are informed of our impending death, will that bring with it denial and anger, or will the years of trying to be God's child give us acceptance and a sense of excitement, knowing that he does not make mistakes, and that his timing is excellent?

'Out of the fullness of his grace he has blessed us all, giving us one blessing after another' (John 1:16). When we have experienced this throughout our lives, how could we doubt that these blessings will continue through the whole dying process?

Written round the dial of a clock in France is the statement: 'One of these hours the Lord is coming'. Will his coming be as Luke describes it – like lightning flashing across the sky, while everyone continues eating and drinking, buying and selling, planting and building and getting married, right up to that time?

What indeed should we be doing instead? Changing our priorities? Becoming more aware of God's presence? Praying? Serving? Loving? Are these the opportunities we have in terminal illness?

Or will he come to me personally as I die – like the thief in the night?

I suppose throughout our lives we have experiences that teach us how to cope with death. Not least of these is caring for the dying. Strangely, when our whole focus of attention is on helping them, it's often they who are of most help to us. More frightening, I think, to find that the first death we ever witness is our own!

If Jesus needed to pray in preparation for his death, surely we do too. Previous generations prayed daily and without morbidness, for a happy and holy death. Do we?

As our departure grows closer, prayer will only flow from us if we have already become fluent. But it is never too late to start, and approaching death can concentrate the mind marvellously on the priorities. Nor is it ever too early to contemplate what those priorities might be, and so adjust our lives accordingly.

What, then, are my own hopes and fears as I contemplate my death? I share my list with you simply to motivate you to make your own, which is bound to be different.

Hopes

1. Ideally, I'd like to have a sense of readiness to die because life has been good and fulfilling and is reaching a point of completion.

2. Part of that readiness includes the practicalities of having completed my will and made arrangements for my funeral.

3. I'd like best to die at home and without too much lack of dignity.

4. I hope to have no regrets, particularly about people I love. Ideally, I will have seen them recently, expressed my deep love for them, said cheerful goodbyes and will have given them the opportunity to have done something really nice for me. This will give them great comfort when I am gone.

5. I hope I will have kept all my promises and done everything that others were hoping I would do for them.

6. I'd like to have the feeling that my children really understood me. My grandchildren, too, if possible.

7. I long for an easy connection with God at this time; that I am blessed with an awareness of his constant presence; that I am guided throughout by him, and have total trust in him. In other words – I cooperate completely with God in the process of dying.

8. I would want the opportunity to share my deep feelings and discoveries with someone and to be able to talk freely about our Lord.

9. I'd love to have happy visitors, who all leave laughing, but carry away with them a strong sense of God's presence, so that they in turn will be helped to die.

10. I hope I can hold on to a sense of excitement and anticipation of God's glory, and somehow be able to share that with all who care for me, that they too will glimpse that glory.

11. I hope I will frequently be helped to focus on Jesus, by being prayed for, over and with, easily and unself-consciously.

12. I'd like to be treated as a perfectly normal, intelligent human being throughout any terminal illness, having everything explained to me, including what I will have to face, and to be consulted about any treatment.

13. Nicest of all would be to come in from the garden one warm, sunny afternoon, sit down, tired but content, giving praise and thanks to God, and die.

14. However I experience the preparation for death, I'd like to slip away without too much fuss at the very end. I do not at all mind the prospect of being on my own, but if someone else needs to be with me for their own peace of mind, then that's okay too.

15. I hope that those I leave behind will be well able to cope without me.

16. I hope they will *celebrate* my death with a deep sense of peace and rightness.

Those are my idealistic hopes!

Now for my fears!

Fears

1. I am frightened by the prospect of excessive pain. A long, slow, painful death would be most fearful.

2. I dread the indignity, loss of personality and helplessness which can mark the ending of life.

3. I do not want to be suspended from life-supporting tubes for weeks on end, or depend on any other way of being kept nominally alive unnecessarily.

4. I would thank no one for rescuing me, e.g. from a fire, simply to face years of mutilated agony.

5. I dread being trapped immobile inside a coma and unable to communicate, while hearing others talk dispassionately about me.

6. I have a deep-seated fear of drowning.

7. I don't want to make an exhibition of myself as I die.

8. I don't want to cause awkward problems like dying on holiday.

9. I'd rather not be among strangers, particularly those who are scared of death and would much rather not be with me.

10. I hope I don't carry any aching regrets to the grave (the 'if only ...' syndrome).

11. I particularly hope I haven't just quarrelled with someone, however trivial the contention.

12. I don't want to be caught with the house like a tip or more than usually shabbily dressed (the 'raggy knicker' syndrome!)

13. I'd hate to be a tedious burden for any length of time to those whose love and strong sense of duty wouldn't allow them to hand me over to the care of others.

14. An accident, provided I was dead on arrival, would be okay, but to be caught in a disaster brings out fears and self-doubts about courage and selflessness.

15. To be the victim of some deliberate violence would be terrifying – facing naked evil in human beings. But this was what Christ had to do.

16. Most fearful of all would be to share Christ's experience of seeming to be rejected by God himself. [Spare me that, O Lord! I'm too much of a child. I'll need your hand to hold every step of the way through dying. Lord, do not put me to that test! You have promised 'I will be with you'. I need you, Lord!]

'Do not be afraid.' I want to live my life according to that, and die according to that. But I know full well that we cannot dodge our Gethsemane! Maybe we have to experience the desolation of God letting go of us – if only momentarily, and if only to experience the ecstasy of being reheld.

Looking again at my list, so much of it stems from trivial pride, and maybe that's where my serious personal preparation for death must begin, but there are certain things we can do to make our hopes become more realistic.

1. A sense of readiness
'I have shown your glory on earth; I have finished the work you gave me to do' (John 17:4). Would that we could say the same thing when we come to the end of our lives. What is the work God wants us to do? Have we discerned it yet? Surely, however young or healthy we are, there is some urgency about discerning the work that God wants us to do. How else can we hope to finish it? We cannot discern if we fail to find time to listen to God in prayer and in his word.

'Give glory to your Son, so that the Son may give glory to you' (John 17:1). So Jesus' death gives glory to both the Father and the Son. If we pray that prayer, will we too receive God's glory, and through our death be able to give glory to God? So our death could be full of glory?

'Happy are those who have been invited to the wedding-feast of the Lamb' (Revelation 19:9). And wise are those who are prepared for the invitation!

'So then, let us purify ourselves from everything that makes body or soul unclean, and let us be completely holy by living in awe of God' (2 Corinthians 7:1), from now on!

Abraham, in obedience, left his own country without knowing where he was going – an experience we share when we die. '... there is no permanent city for us here on earth' (Hebrews 13:14), but don't we often behave as if our roots are here for ever? Instead, we are to believe in the Kingdom of God and be eager to be there when invited. Until then, we have work to get on with.

2. Relationships with others
Jesus spoke very little as he prepared to die. He had said all he wanted to say well before, though John's Gospel gives us

the feeling of our Lord packing as much detail as possible into his final summary of how we are to live.

We are to love God and love our neighbour. Were we to strive to do this for the rest of our days, regardless of what lies behind us, we could make no better preparation for our own death, be it sudden or anticipated. 'Your life must be controlled by love' (Ephesians 5:2), and so too our dying.

'I pray that your love will keep on growing more and more, together with true knowledge and perfect judgement ... Then you will be free from all impurity and blame on the Day of Christ' (Philippians 1:9-10). The whole process of decision-making in our lives, particularly how we treat other people, should be influenced by that Day of Christ.

Surely it is also necessary that we constantly tell people that we love them. We do not want to come to the point of death and find things unsaid, perhaps leaving behind many hurtful misapprehensions. There is a certain urgency to put right any wrongs we may have caused or allowed to happen.

I want to be open with my loved ones, discuss my attitude to death and even, at times, pray together about our mutual acceptance of death, long before it is imminent. This way I hope that the difficult moment of sharing the news of terminal illness will be eased – that it will be almost familiar ground.

'The same rules you use to judge others will be used by God to judge you – but with even greater severity' (Mark 4:24). Facing death is a time to forgive, heal past injuries and get relationships right. And if that is how we want to face death, surely it would be a good way to live life. We could live life excusing people from their mistakes. We all make them. Indeed, we can't learn much without them.

Viewed from that angle, we can even come to value people *for* their mistakes.

3. Thankfulness
Will we return to the Lord, as one of the ten lepers did, thanking him for his many graces and blessings? There is so much

that we take for granted in our daily lives, for which we should be giving God constant praise and thanks. His Holy Spirit brings awareness of all that we owe him. '... we have received the Spirit sent by God, so that we may know all that God has given us' (1 Corinthians 2:12).

We, in return, have so little to give. Jesus noticed '... a very poor woman dropping in two little copper coins ... she, poor as she is, gave all she had to live on' (Luke 21:2-4).

In a way, as we approach death, we can give God little more than two copper coins – we have so little of value to offer. Yet we know he will accept our gift with joy, and even respect.

4. Co-operation

Paul said, 'We felt that the death sentence had been passed on us. But this happened so that we should rely, not on ourselves, but only on God, who raises the dead' (2 Corinthians 1:9). As we feel we are approaching death, there is little else for us to do other than rely entirely on God – whatever we have previously done.

The pain and anguish of preparing for death will be accompanied by God's strength. We have new experiences ahead of us. As we come to meet them – God will already be there. Everything that happens to us will be so that we can learn something new from God.

Familiarity with his Word and his ways will help us to interpret what is happening to us. [Lord, help us to co-operate fully with you. Teach us to listen attentively. Make our impending death sharpen our hearing, our perception and our vision.]

'We live in union with the true God – in union with his Son Jesus Christ. This is the true God, and this is eternal life' (1 John 5:20). So in one sense, we have already embarked on our eternal life!

5. Honesty

'If someone thinks he is somebody when really he is nobody, he is only deceiving himself.' When facing death, the last thing we want to do is to deceive ourselves. But isn't this exactly what silly pride is?

Maybe, as we prepare, we come to face our true selves for the first time. Perhaps this causes us to be in shock! At this point of realisation, we have to remember that God has *always known our true selves, loves us still, and always will*, even though we may in fact be repulsed by ourselves! This is a logic that I find very comforting at moments of self-illumination.

There are reasons why God allows us to see ourselves at times through his eyes. Painful as this can be, it is, in fact, a superbly co-operative act of God. We will survive the experience.

Peter said, 'I am ready to die for you!' (John 13:37), but in fact he wasn't! He dodged the merest hint of it, just like the rest of us. But in time, with the Holy Spirit within him, he became ready and submitted to God's choice of time and circumstances. We too have need of the Holy Spirit to face our own inevitable and unique death with willingness. God will be as creative about our death as he has been about our lives. It will be special if we work with him.

Of course, we will be anxious at times, afraid of pain and suffering, troubled about being tested – all this is human frailty and Jesus has experienced all that too. It is how we cope with our vunerability that marks us out as believing, trusting Christians.

We are meant to accept the difficulties and know we are safe in God's care. He doesn't want us to dodge the storm, but to accept that the consequences are according to his will, including death. That death is merely the junction between this life and life with him.

'Jesus stood up and commanded the wind, "Be quiet!" and he said to the waves, "Be still!" The wind died down, and there was a great calm. Then Jesus said to his disciples, "Why are you frightened? Have you still no faith?"' (Mark 4:39-40).

How death and dying tests our trust in God!

And through all this trauma we are told: 'You must shine among them like the stars lighting up the sky' (Philippians 2:15). A star! – No teeth! No hair! Deaf and blind and going senile and still shining! And most of us are lucky enough to know someone who has managed to do just that!

To a Christian then, the only true measure of the success of our lives is the quality of our death. Why do we fight it? Fear it? Cover ourselves in black and tears?

Why do we not understand God's promises? Believe in them? Rejoice in them? Anticipate that joy all our lives?

Almighty God, forgive us our lack of faith. Our lack of awareness. Our lack of imagination!

God's glory! This is what our departed loved ones are already experiencing! This is what our departing loved ones are approaching! This is what we ourselves can hope for!

Alleluia! Alleluia! Alleluia! We have a wonderful Creator! He has given us our Resurrection!

Practicalities

With our feet still firmly planted on this earth, we look at the practical ways that we can be ready for death – not for our own sakes, but to make it easier for our loved ones to cope with our death.

Before Jesus died, he made simple provision for those he loved specially. To Mary he said, 'He is your son', and to John he said, 'She is your mother' (John 19:26,27), and although this has been given the significance of Mary becoming mother to us all, it also gave her protection and purpose in her own life.

Within the emotional confusion of any death, there are certain things which have to be done by those left behind. In my experience, one of the most worrying practical things is finding all the right pieces of paper.

The kindest thing to do is to gather together all the appropriate information and always keep it together, in a box, a case or file. Let all the family and the executors know exactly what you have done and where it is kept. Take them through it at some unemotional time and in a very practical way. Be sure they listen! All too easily they joke or dodge the information. (I know, I've done it! But that was my inadequacy and embarrassment. I should have recognised the needs of the one who wanted to tell me. We learn some things the hard way!)

What should be in the black box?
1. Guidance on what to do when you die. (Contact the doctor for a death certificate. He will advise on whether the police or the coroner must also be contacted, and arrange what to do with the body. Then the death must be registered.)
2. The name and telephone number of the funeral director, perhaps giving guidance on some limit to cost.
3. Birth and marriage certificates.
4. Name, address and telephone number of your solicitor.
5. All insurance policies for life, house and car.
6. List of regular payments and how, when and where these are paid (mortgage; gas; electricity; tax; rent; rates; insurances; credit card accounts etc.).
7. Social insurance number and any professional reference numbers.
8. Name, address and telephone number of any business contacts that have to be made.
9. The self-employed should leave careful guidance regarding all business contracts.
10. Name, address and telephone number of all those you would wish to be notified of your death, including clubs, associations and societies.
11. Building society and bank accounts; pension book and any other source of money, particularly how to obtain money for immediate needs.
12. Information on any special allowances, such as disability.

13. Guidance for funeral arrangements, including any provision such as the number and certificate for any owned burial plot.

14. Guidance for the funeral service.

15. An updated will.

Doubtless there are other things that you would like to add. I intend putting in a letter to each of my loved ones, letting them know how much I valued each of them in a special way. Although they probably know it all, it will be a good time to have that knowledge reinforced.

As to the funeral service – I want mine to be an unashamed, full blast celebration.

If I go tomorrow, I have had a thoroughly well blessed life, so I want all who have shared in it to share in the wholehearted thanks for it. God has showered blessings upon me, and I want 'thank you' to be the predominant prayer.

I want white vestments, singing, flowers and all the outward signs of celebration, because I will have taken the most exciting journey of my life (and all who know me well, know how excited I can get!). I will already have met God. I will already know his incredible love, his light, his almightiness. And – because of my sins – whatever technical delays there may be between death and wholeness within God – I will already have started on that metamorphosis.

Hopefully, the prayers of the community will speed me into his Kingdom. Jesus Christ will already have asked for just that. 'I pray for ... those you gave me, for they belong to you' (John 17:9).

Don't be anxious for me when I have such a perfect advocate. I belong to God. His Kingdom is my home. Rejoice with me, please, for I am where I belong. Alleluia! Alleluia!

Then I want all my friends to go home together, have the kettle on for those who have gone to the graveside, make some sandwiches and settle down to tell each other all the funny stories they can remember against me. That will cut me down to an appropriate size and the day will end in laughter as well as tears.

And so it must be if I am the one left to mourn. The physical body that we are letting go of is releasing the spirit to be free and whole in God. From within the agony of our broken hearts, we have to try to touch the glory of God that is being shared with the one we love.

Those who have celebrated life will be given the strength and the vision to celebrate eternal life, even at this time.

Two further suggestions for funeral arrangements:

1. At the back of the church, put up a recent photograph of the one who has died. So often we recognise people by sight rather than by name. This way we attract the prayers of every passing acquaintance.

2. Put an open book at the back of the church for all to sign as they come or go from the funeral service. It is a great consolation to know that so many friends were there to support us with their prayers, yet we can be so distraught at such times that we register nothing of their presence.

As to the will – we were recently bereaved and had to dismantle a home at a time when my two daughters were both struggling to set up their homes. They acquired so many useful bits and pieces that they felt quite guilty. But, since then, they have both commented on how frequently, through everyday chores, they are reminded of their benefactor.

This surely would be nice to have happen to us, so all our loved ones and friends, particularly the young, can be encouraged to take the everyday things. These will be constant reminders. It also saves us inflicting quite the wrong things on people who are too polite to refuse them. After all, we're often attracted by the silly things rather than the valuable – that's supposing anything is left in the house after the great 'letting go'!

Talking over things like this, while in a happy and healthy

mood, helps those we talk with to come to terms with our inevitable death. The less taboo the subject, the more we help them.

I certainly hope that by the time I die, I am well on in my clearing-out operation. Right at the moment, my descendants would have to get a skip just to clear the attic. There is a great sadness in reducing someone's whole history into a stack of black bags. It would be kinder to do it for them, besides saving them a million trivial decisions about totally unimportant things, like rubber bands, book lists, anniversary cards, unenthusiastic felt-tipped pens, scraps of material and ribbons, dull stones and shells from forgotten beaches, plus the sand, and enough pins, needles and threads to sew up all the skirts of the nation.

Why do I do it? And continue to do it even as I begin to empty out drawers? Am I alone in this economical mania?

The Ethiopians aren't troubled in this way, which shows the wisdom of selling all and giving to the poor!

45

4

SIN

Do we fear death because we are sinners?

We have been created to walk with God, but our sins keep us at a distance from him. Even so, God loves us so ardently that in spite of our sins, he has taken the initiative to heal the rift. He has given us the right to become his children. God will never abandon his children, however wayward, certainly not at the point of death.

He knows us, and understands us through and through. 'There is nothing that can be hidden from God; everything in all creation is exposed and lies open before his eyes' (Hebrews 4:13). He knows *why* we sin, far better than we do ourselves. He sees our weaknesses; the pressures we are under; the deprivations we suffer; the influences that have distorted us and the others who have involved us in sin.

In spite of all this knowledge, he has chosen us! '... you are the chosen race ... God's own people... (he) called you out of darkness into his own marvellous light ... now you have received his mercy' (1 Peter 2:9-10).

He has chosen to give us the gift of faith. He does not force this down our throats (nor can we force it on others). It is on offer to us. To some he seems to give it on a plate, easy to accept, attractive, obvious. Others, he allows to struggle for years. From others, he appears to snatch away their intellectual belief for a time. To more – he doesn't seem to reveal himself at all throughout their life on earth.

This is a great puzzle to us, who do not have God's perspective or purpose. We can only trust God. Who is to receive the gift of faith, and when, is entirely God's choice. Like Rebecca's two sons, 'God's choice was based on his call, and not on anything they had done' (Romans 9:12). God has every right to choose. '... the man who makes the pots has the right to use the clay as he wishes' (Romans 9:21).

We are entirely dependent upon God's mercy. 'It is not that we have loved God, but that he loved us' (1 John 4:10). He *does* choose and he has chosen *us*. Once we become aware of God's choice, we do have to make some response, as a farmer has to cleanse his soil in preparation for the crop.

'Get the road ready for the Lord; make a straight path for him to travel!', Isaiah directed. We have to straighten ourselves out for the coming of Christ. We are to be open to God, then his Holy Spirit will direct us away from sin. And turning from sin means turning to face God – good practice for when we die.

We are to listen to him, trying to understand his personal message to us, rooting it deep in our being, working to cultivate a sensitive and educated conscience, because this is the litmus paper for discerning God's will for us on earth.

All this is difficult work, but we never work alone on this preparation – God is with us – Jesus Christ, Son of the living God. He is with us, working to make a success of our life's work for him. He came to love us, teach us, heal us, make the Father known to us, and by his death, to take away our sins. '... the Lamb of God, who takes away the sin of the world!' (John 1:29).

Jesus *has* taken away our sins – yesterday's, today's and tomorrow's sins. He *has* put us right with God. That is what we can celebrate today. We are no longer condemned by our sins. '... everyone has sinned. ... But by the free gift of God's grace all are put right with him through Jesus Christ' (Romans 3:23-4). *All* people are put right with God!

'Christ himself is the means by which our sins are forgiven, and not our sins only, but also the sins of everyone' (1 John 2:2). He does not judge us. Instead he loves us and saves us. He is on our side. We will certainly have him by our side to rescue us as we die.

'God did not send his Son into the world to be its judge, but to be its saviour' (John 3:17).

47

'I pass judgement on no one' (John 8:15).

And so – incredible as this seems to us sinners – he *wants* to be with us where we are weakest. He doesn't want to avoid our sinfulness. He comes to us *because* we are sinners, as he sought out Mary Magdalene. Isn't that lovely! 'The Son of Man came to seek and to save the lost' (Luke 19:10).

He *wants* to help us, heal us and support us. He may enjoy our good points, but our badness is what concerns him; attracts his attention; calls out to his love – because we are his Body.

In my own human body, if I suffer a boil on the back of my hand, I do not chop my hand off! Instead, I treat it with constant care and attention until it is better. My own head would certainly concentrate on the offending part of my body.

Christ is the head of his Body. Those of us who are diseased with sin attract his special attention. This is a marvellous comfort to me, a sinner!

Jesus Christ wants to be with our worst parts. He will not force his way there. He waits patiently to be invited. Once invited, he lavishes his care upon us until we are healed. He delights in our company until through him '... we become God's holy people and are set free' (1 Corinthians 1:30).

We cannot earn this. We do not deserve it. It is a free gift from God – the only genuine 'free offer' this side of the grave! We ARE REDEEMED! Jesus was condemned instead of Barabbas. He was let off. So are we!

'Who will accuse God's chosen people? God himself declares them not guilty!' (Romans 8:33).

'Our sins are forgiven' (Ephesians 1:7).

How on earth do we respond to the enormity of this generous offer?

1. WE BELIEVE – '... everyone who believes in him will have their sins forgiven through the power of his name' (Acts 10:43). Faith that Jesus is able and wants to heal us of our

sins, is what is required on our side. We do not work alone on becoming holy – nor does Jesus!

2. WE ACCEPT – with awe and wonder, the gift of daily reconciliation that the Lord offers to those who believe.

3. WE THANK AND PRAISE HIM – That is the least we can do. We can offer him no gift to equal his. We can only acknowledge his generosity. 'How great is the grace of God, which he gave to us in such large measure' (Ephesians 1:7-8). 'Let us praise God for his glorious grace, for the free gift he gave us in his dear Son!' (Ephesians 1:6).

4. WE REPENT – 'Wash your hands,you sinners! Purify your hearts,you hypocrites! Be sorrowful, cry, and weep; change your laughter into crying, your joy into gloom! Humble yourselves before the Lord, and he will lift you up' (James 4:8-10). It is important that we feel this remorse for our sins. It is equally important that we move through repentance to experience being lifted up. Then the angels rejoice with us. '... the angels of God rejoice over one sinner who repents' (Luke 15:10). If we repent and accept God's loving forgiveness, from that point onwards – *we are prepared for death!*

5. WE TURN FROM OUR SINS – According to Matthew's Gospel, Jesus' first message was 'Turn away from your sins, because the Kingdom of heaven is near!' (Matthew 4:17). We have consciously to reject our sinful ways because of God's love for us.

6. WE IMITATE HIM – '... put on the new self, which is created in God's likeness and reveals itself in the true life that is upright and holy' (Ephesians 4:24). And here we are, attempting to feel as he feels, think as he thinks, perceive as he perceives, and so become totally open to the Father's will.

7. WE REJOICE IN OUR WEAKNESS – so that even as we are in the process of failing to become Christ-like, we can learn to submit more and more to his take-over bid for us. 'My grace is all you need, for my power is greatest when you are weak' (2 Corinthians 12:9).

8. WE LOVE – 'Do those things that will show that you have turned from your sins' (Luke 3:8). That is, love God and love each other with the same unconditional love. That way, our faith becomes experiential rather than merely notional.

9. WE OBEY – 'If you love me, you will obey my commandments'; 'If you obey my teaching, you are really my disciples; you will know the truth, and the truth will set you free!' (John 8:31-32).

10. WE SHARE – We must pass on the message we have been given, to as much of the world as we can touch. '... in his name the message about repentance and the forgiveness of sins must be preached to all nations' (Luke 24:47). We are not meant to hug to ourselves the knowledge of our redemption. It is not a secret message to us alone. Jesus came to save all. All need to know, then they too can respond.

11. WE FORGIVE – Terminal illness is a key time to forgive all those whom we imagine have offended us. 'If you forgive others the wrongs they have done to you, your Father in heaven will also forgive you' (Matthew 6:14). What a simple way to claim God's forgiveness, and how reasonable to do it *now*, rather than savouring another's guilt for one more day.

12. WE SERVE – 'The servant does not deserve thanks for obeying orders, does he? It is the same with you' (Luke 17:9-10). Has sin brought about our lost sense of servanthood? Are we so hung up on equal rights and so bent on pleasure, that we cannot stomach being a servant to another? How sad if this is true. To serve the weak, the poor, the inadequate, is our purpose for living. To love and serve them is to love and serve Christ.

13. WE LISTEN TO HIM – 'Listen! I stand at the door and knock; if anyone hears my voice and opens the door, I will come into his house and eat with him, and he will eat with me' (Revelation 3:20).

We are more likely to believe in 'the God who declares the guilty innocent' (Romans 4:5), if we have made every effort to open the door to him, listened to his word and pondered over all that he chooses to reveal to us.

14. WE NEED NOT FEAR DEATH – When we die, Christ will bring us before the Father, purified and holy – simply because he loves us. 'Nor does the Father himself judge anyone. He has given his Son the full right to judge...' (John 5:22). They both opt out of judging! They love us too much.

Daily, if we choose to, we can be forgiven and made new by our Saviour Jesus Christ. We are not dependent upon any church, or priest or sacrament – but upon Christ alone! The church or priest may be able to help us come to true repentance and, through the Sacrament of Reconciliation, God's grace will strengthen our resolve to turn from our sins, but Christ alone removes the guilt of those sins. He took them upon himself at Calvary.

Not to respond to this loving Jesus – is sin!

If we do *not* believe, repent, turn from sin; if we fail to praise and thank God; if we do not love him and his people and serve them at every opportunity; if we refuse to forgive; if we fail to share his word with those around us who want to hear it; if we deliberately choose not to listen to him – then we fail to accept his love and forgiveness, and so we reject his redemption. All this is sin!

Yet – it is the sinner whom our Lord and Saviour seeks out. He chooses to be with sinners. That is where his work is.

It is the hardest thing in the world to shake off our God. Our God wants us and he *will* win. At death he will claim us as his own.

Then why bother striving for holiness while we are alive on earth?

Simply to be a joy to God. To become his obedient instrument in his plan of salvation for the world.

How could we choose to serve him meanly when we come to realise his incredible generosity?

Is ours the sin of being lukewarm? Of being meagre in

51

love? Of loving self above all else? God forgive us our sins, and be with us in our weakness.

When I need encouragement, I look at Peter – he rarely understood what our Lord was getting at. He was full of swagger and bluster. When put to the test, he failed. But Jesus told him not to worry about either his weaknesses or his sins – they were forgiven. Instead, he had to accept the power of the Spirit and get on with God's work.

In our very weakest moments – when we are close to death – the Power of the Spirit will be at its strongest within us.

Christ will plead for us.

He has taken away our sins.

Accept and believe! The choice is ours! This dangerous free will! Choose life, and choose it *now*.

5

SUFFERING

'My heart is stricken within me,
death's terror is on me,
trembling and fear fall upon me
and horror overwhelms me' (Psalm 54:5-6).

There are millions of people better than I who have struggled with the problem of suffering in relation to our loving God. I can only ask questions and make tentative suggestions in the hope that the Holy Spirit will give each one of us the insights necessary for our individual needs.

Also, there are so many possible sufferings of body, mind and spirit that it is rather ridiculous to lump them all together, but out of consideration for the length of this chapter, that is exactly what I have done.

We are all capable of inflicting suffering of all kinds, both on ourselves and others, through our passions, our greed, jealousy, anger, carelessness, ignorance, indifference, insensitivity, etc. So we suffer because of our sins and the sins of others. Without sin, there would be no suffering. Suffering, therefore, cannot originate in God, though he certainly does allow it.

If we repent, Jesus has promised to remove the guilt of our sins. He never promised to remove our suffering. Therefore, there must be purpose in that suffering.

On the other hand, while Jesus was on earth, he always eased the suffering of those he met. He never said – 'Because you are sinful you must suffer'. Nor even – 'Put up with your suffering for the glory of God'.

The most problematic of all sufferings are those of the young and the innocent. But here, surely, is suffering most like Christ's – undeserved! It is to Christ's passion then, that we must look for some understanding of the value of our own suffering.

Jesus declared that '... the Son of Man *must* suffer much' (Mark 8:31; my emphasis), and when Peter protested against this, Jesus rounded on him in no uncertain terms: 'Get away from me, Satan!' (Mark 8:33). Indeed, it would have been disastrous for humankind if Peter had deterred Jesus from his crucifixion and death! Jesus *had* to suffer. Even *chose* to suffer. Must we also choose to?

'If anyone wants to come with me, he must forget self, carry his cross and follow me' (Mark 8:34).

Jesus even said: 'Now my heart is troubled ... But that is why I came – so that I might go through this hour of suffering' (John 12:27).

So all that our Lord did throughout his lifetime was subordinate to his suffering. He became human primarily to suffer for us!

Is our suffering also the most important aspect of our presence on earth? Can it also be a gift to humankind? Or could it be, if we knew how to make it so?

'... the cup of suffering which my Father has given me' (John 18:11). This cup Jesus accepted willingly, although he was afraid of it. He had no resentment of it. No comment about it being undeserved. He accepted it eagerly, seeing it as his greatest contribution to humankind.

Are we too meant to embrace suffering, seeing it as of far greater worth than any of our perceived successes? That is certainly worth pondering!

In his anguish, Jesus calls out, 'Father, if you will, take this cup of suffering away from me. Not my will, however, but your will be done' (Luke 22:42). This needs to be our regular prayer too, not only on our lips, but felt in our hearts, long before our final suffering. This needs practice.

Even Jesus, at this point in his passion, looks for support. His disciples failed him, but maybe others down the ages were in some way able to give him the solace of knowing that they were prepared to share his heavy burden. Maybe these are the people who suffer out of all proportion to the rest of us, yet remain full of the Lord's peace and joy. Is that their special vocation? Perhaps we too have something to contribute to the solace he sought.

That means that at our Gethsemane, when we are weak and suffering, we have the greatest gift for Jesus – our willingness to share his passion. At that point too, others may be prepared to offer their suffering to relieve our agony. How interlinked we all are, and prayer draws Christ into this entanglement.

He understands every angle of our suffering, because he himself experienced the tremendous weight of pain – physical, mental and emotional. 'Grief and anguish came over him, and he said to them, "The sorrow in my heart is so great that it almost crushes me"' (Matthew 26:37-38). Because of this, we know that Jesus understands the very depth of our deepest depression. He has been even lower – 'My God, my God, why did you abandon me?' (Matthew 27:46).

Any degradation that we may experience cannot equal that of God's Son being pinned to a criminal's cross. Any rejection that is inflicted upon us, cannot match the sense of rejection that Jesus must have had. Even as he gave his all, he knew the world would continue to turn against him.

Whatever depth we reach, we will find Christ already there. Because he is there, God's glory is there too.

Jesus suffered as he did to save humankind, and through his obedience gave glory to God. We are surely meant to imitate this motivation. Personally, I know it will take me a lifetime of being moulded by the Lord's hands before I can even begin to do this. I have to change so much! There is a world of difference between knowing with the mind and accepting with the heart, and even my mind is struggling to accept!

But suffering itself can tutor us. Amongst many things, we

discover our limitations, and our total dependence upon God. It counters our arrogance; it illustrates how vulnerable we are, stirring us out of a false sense of our own dignity, self-sufficiency, self-importance and complacency. For those who wish to accept them, there are many fruits of suffering, including humility and courage.

Do we learn most about God's love for us through our own suffering? Particularly if we suffer rejection? Indeed, could we ever truly appreciate the Redemption without experiencing suffering ourselves?

If we imitate Christ's attitude to his death, then we suffer and die for others. In so doing, we please God. Is this our role – our purpose in life?

My God, how wrong I have got my priorities!

'... take your part in suffering for the Good News, as God gives you the strength to do it' (2 Timothy 1:8).

Maybe it is through our suffering that we will eventually become totally obedient to the will of God, as Jesus himself did: '...even though he was God's Son, he learnt through his sufferings to be obedient' (Hebrews 5:8). As we, too, somehow must become obedient.

And there are many promised compensations for our sufferings: '... what we suffer ... cannot be compared at all with the glory that is going to be revealed to us' (Romans 8:18); '... this small and temporary trouble we suffer will bring us a tremendous and eternal glory, much greater than the trouble' (2 Corinthians 4:17).

This may help us to see past our suffering to the waiting Lord. This way we get the whole experience into perspective. 'For we fix our attention, not on things that are seen, but on things that are unseen. What can be seen lasts only for a time, but what cannot be seen lasts for ever' (2 Corinthians 4:18). That long-distance focus on the Kingdom of God.

'... if we share Christ's suffering, we will also share his glory' (Romans 8:17). *There's* motivation not to dodge suffering.

'Don't be afraid of anything you are about to suffer. ... Be faithful to me, even if it means death, and I will give you life as your prize of victory' (Revelation 2:10).

'Just as we have a share in Christ's many sufferings, so also through Christ we share in God's great help' (2 Corinthians 1:5).

'... after you have suffered for a little while, the God of all grace, who calls you to share his eternal glory in union with Christ, will himself perfect you and give you firmness, strength, and a sure foundation' (l Peter 5:10). We will experience our resurrection, bringing us '... into God's presence as a mature individual in union with Christ' (Colossians 1:28).

'God will bless you ... if you endure the pain of undeserved suffering *because you are conscious of his will*' (l Peter 2:19; emphasis mine).

'... do not be surprised at the painful test you are suffering, as though something unusual were happening to you. Rather be glad that you are sharing Christ's sufferings, so that you may be full of joy when his glory is revealed' (l Peter 4:12-13).

Rejoice in our own sufferings! What a difficult concept, but over and over again, in the New Testament, we are urged to do just that.

'... consider yourselves fortunate when all kinds of trials come your way, for you know that when your faith succeeds in facing such trials, the result is the ability to endure. Make sure that your endurance carries you all the way without failing, so that you may be perfect and complete, lacking nothing' (James 1:2-4).

'Happy is the person who remains faithful under trials, because when he succeeds in passing such a test, he will receive as his reward the life which God has promised to those who love him' (James 1:12).

'... if you endure suffering even when you have done right, God will bless you for it. *It was to this that God called you*, for Christ himself suffered for you and left you an example' (l Peter 2:20-21; emphasis mine).

So suffering is the high point of our spiritual lives? Or could be?

And from the opposite angle, those who suffer are to be greatly treasured, for they are doing their greatest work for humankind. In caring for them, we share a little in their work. Maybe, by being involved in their suffering, we can help them to see its purpose.

Think of the millions of silent sufferers. Many are alone: prisoners; alcoholics; the poor; the illiterate; the mentally damaged; the physically handicapped; the disfigured; AIDS victims; unwanted refugees; drug addicts; the elderly, and so on.

Yet, as we have seen, it is these sufferers whom we should be valuing far more than the achievers.

Maybe the only way that many sufferers can tolerate their pain is by being shown how much they are valued. And maybe they need our help to put their suffering into God's care. 'For you have been given the privilege of serving Christ, not only by believing in him, but also by suffering for him' (Philippians 1:29).

The privilege of suffering! Now there's a puzzle to our modern ears! Eventually, as we struggle with it, we will be helped with the puzzle. 'The Helper will come – the Spirit, who reveals the truth about God' (John 15:26). '...he will lead you into all the truth' (John 16:13).

For certain, God is in this mystery of suffering. A mystery to be entered into rather than to be solved. Maybe part of our suffering has to be that we can never fully understand – only endure in faith. 'For what seems to be God's foolishness is wiser than human wisdom, and what seems to be God's weakness is stronger than human strength' (l Corinthians 1:25).

'I strove to fathom this problem,
too hard for my mind to understand,
until I pierced the mysteries of God' (Psalm 72:16-17).

And that's part of the difficulty, isn't it, that we don't have God's perspective on things.

We are so often inappropriately sad. At a time of God's great glory, we are found weeping, like Martha and Mary for Lazarus, and Mary Magdalene for Jesus. Maybe our lowest ebb of pain and desolation immediately precedes the time of God's glory being shown in us? As if we have to do a total emptying to the depth of ourselves, before we can share in that glory. Even Jesus on the Cross hit rock bottom just before his greatest triumph was accomplished. Paul, on the road to Damascus, became totally helpless, before being filled with the Holy Spirit.

Our suffering may follow the same pattern, particularly if we have a terminal illness, where death is the complete emptying out.

A priest has explained to me that sometimes, as devout Christians approach death, their strong faith seems to falter. This surely parallels the Lord's feeling of desolation that evoked the cry: 'My God, my God, why did you abandon me?' (Mark 15:34)

If we have this terrifying experience, all we can do is hang on with blind faith, and cling to the support of those who care and pray for us. But, apparently, the person who is suffering this way rarely mentions this particular agony, from some sense of guilt, or a desire to avoid distressing those around them. However, it's a recognised spiritual phenomenon, well documented in the life of St Thérèse of Lisieux, who spent fifteen months in such pain.

This is the final purification, it is believed. When this trial is over, the one who is sick very often dies soon after.

Yes, from God's point of view, we must so often be inappropriately sad as our loved ones go through their different experiences of death, and on to participate in God's glory. But keep in mind the meaning of glory!

'When a woman is about to give birth, she is sad because her hour of suffering has come; but when the baby is born, she

59

forgets her suffering' (John 16:21). Now there is an emptying-out experience! But there are women who go very cheerfully into labour in high anticipation of the joy of a new-born baby. Should we tackle pain similarly? Can we learn to relax in our suffering as we can learn to control birth pangs to a certain extent? If we put our pain into God's care for his use, trusting him not to over-test us, do we eliminate fear, tensions and resentments? Could all our suffering be part of the birth pangs of creation evolving in God's hands? Is pain inevitable for creation?

If we artificially smother, avoid or dodge pain, do we also, in some way, smother something in creation? Do we lose out on our own creativity? The bland are not usually creative people. Is pain the price that has to be paid for being creative? Is pain the matter that God creates from? Is there some choice in there somewhere to be either creative or passive?

Do we build on to the creative act of Christ's Redemption? But surely Christ's sacrifice was complete, lacking nothing, and all other suffering petty and ridiculous in comparison? Yet it is God's nature to value our trivia and so give value to that minuteness.

'... a man from Cyrene named Simon ... the soldiers forced him to carry Jesus' cross' (Matthew 27:32). Is this saying that Jesus *couldn't* do it entirely on his own? He *needs* our help? Simon represents us?

It seems unlikely that Christ's Redemption could be lacking in anything, yet it is so much the way of Christ – to allow us to become involved in all that he does. Even to the point of being co-bearers of the sins of the world? Paul certainly felt so: '... by means of my physical sufferings I am helping to complete what still remains of Christ's sufferings on behalf of his body, the church' (Colossians 1:24).

Maybe if we accept our suffering joyfully, we give some slight relief to Jesus at the time of his Crucifixion. Perhaps that way we take on some responsibility for the guilt of our own sins?

Think of the restraint of the Father and the Son, who could have called on twelve armies of angels – and didn't! When Jesus asked that the cup of suffering be taken from him – how close did the Father come to granting his plea? Does God suffer whenever he resists a request like that?

Christ, living in our suffering selves – is he suffering still? Or did his suffering end at Calvary? Maybe God still suffers for our sinfulness.

Suffering is certainly a mystery. We can pray about it and pray through it. We can ponder and question and search the will of God, but often, in the end, we simply have to submit to it, in humble recognition of our vulnerable humanity. We are, after all, designed to be his suffering servants, so pain should be no surprise.

Jesus warns us: 'The world will make you suffer' (John 16:33), and Paul warns Timothy: 'Everyone who wants to live a godly life in union with Christ Jesus will be persecuted' (2 Timothy 3:12). It seems to be the inevitable consequence of being God's own.

'In everything we do we show that we are God's servants by patiently enduring troubles, hardships, and difficulties' (2 Corinthians 6:4). And isn't this exactly what we have to do as we come face to face with terminal illness? Might suffering sometimes be like unpalatable medicine, something we are better for having taken?

Personally, pain is inclined to focus my attention intensely upon myself. Are we meant to find a way of focusing on Christ, so that we move through our suffering to him and with him? Does it become a very special sort of prayer experience then? A deep meditation on Christ's Passion? And through recognising Christ's agony, do we get our own pain into perspective?

Others may be helped more by looking beyond his suffering and have eyes only for the Resurrected Christ, and so to our own reflected, glorious resurrection.

Through knowing Christ, Paul gained great motivation

for accepting suffering: 'All I want is to know Christ and to experience the power of his resurrection, to share in his sufferings and become like him in his death, in the hope that I myself will be raised from death to life' (Philippians 3:10-11).

If it is all part of God's plan, then suffering must have great value – provided we offer it to him. As we have discovered, God can use our suffering for the good of all. We are so interdependent anyway, that when one part of the body suffers, so do we all. We are neither meant to suffer alone, nor reap the value of our sufferings for ourselves. 'Take your part in suffering, as a loyal soldier of Christ Jesus' (2 Timothy 2:3).

Perhaps our trials and sorrows are another's passport to the Kingdom? Maybe we can only get into heaven via the suffering of others? Christ's first, but endorsed by others? It fits with God's plan of interdependence.

Are those of us who know Christ asked to contribute our suffering for those who do not know him? Do those closest to God suffer most? Is suffering a privilege that we are invited to join in? (What dangers there could be of taking some kind of spiritual pride in our suffering!)

Do some people suffer through their inability to accept God's love, his blessings, his joy, his peace? Can that suffering be their way back to a rejected God? We cannot know, but we can wonder.

Do illnesses, accidents or emotional turmoils become our opportunities? Our crosses? Are we meant to carry them willingly and with purpose? Do we in fact grumble every resentful step of the way? Or even opt out?

Surely we can only experience the holiness of suffering when we are closely in step with God, yoked to him, so that in fact he shares the load? 'Come to me, all you who are tired from carrying heavy loads, and I will give you rest. Take my yoke and put it on you, and learn from me, because I am gentle and humble in spirit; and you will find rest. For the yoke I will give you is easy, and the load I will put on you is light' (Matthew 11:28).

This implies that God is already pulling the load and we are only asked to give temporary assistance, as Simon of Cyrene was. If the yoke is too heavy, then, it is a sure sign that we are overburdening ourselves in some unnecessary way; or someone else is imposing a burden that we are not meant to carry; or we are refusing assistance from others; or are we refusing God's assistance?

The great consolation through all suffering is the closeness of Christ. He is there when we are in any kind of difficulty. There are many who witness to his intense presence in any disaster. He is attracted, like iron filings to a magnet, to the weak and the suffering. We see it in his visible life on earth, and we have personal experience of it now. The sufferer, like the sinner, attracts the Healer.

As we suffer terminal illness, Christ homes in! This experience alone becomes cause for celebration as all concerned gain heightened spiritual awareness. Not that suffering itself is ever to be glorified, but Christ is vividly present, and through him, our suffering can give glory to God.

There, in the sick room, is dark, holy ground!

Do I even begin to understand the cup of suffering allowed by our loving God? He who gives only good things?

Do I really believe, in my mind and my heart, that suffering can be good for me and has value? That it might be my greatest opportunity on earth? My most valuable gift to humankind? If we don't suffer, are we deprived? No cross, no crown! Am I able to accept all God's blessings with equal joy, including the blessing of sharing in his passion?

God Almighty, help us to get it right. May the Holy Spirit guide us all to that knowledge, understanding and *acceptance*. Lord, help us, above all things, to give you thanks for the priceless gift of your redeeming act, which alone gives value to our pain.

'... make sure that Christ's death on the cross is not robbed of its power' (l Corinthians 1:17). By your holy Cross, O Lord, you have redeemed the world!

In Jesus' act of breaking bread for the four thousand (Matthew 15:35), little became much. One Man, broken on the Cross, redeemed the whole world. Is it the same when we are broken? Lord, please continue to teach us, long after we have stopped puzzling!

Of one thing we can be certain – there will be no suffering in heaven, only the joy and wonder of God's love for us. Even here on earth, our fear of suffering should never be allowed to spoil the present moment of joy!

6

HEALING

'My Father, if it is possible, take this cup of
suffering from me! Yet not what I want, but
what you want' (Matthew 26:39).

This prayer must precede any contemplation of healing. It is
essential that, both as sufferers and carers, we align ourselves to these words.

Healing was the outward sign that Jesus often chose to
show that he had forgiven sins.

Perhaps some of our ills are caused by our lack of repentance for our sins; or our lack of forgiveness for others; or
maybe another's lack of forgiveness; or even an inability to
accept forgiveness. Many sores fester where hatred is cher-
ished.

One person's greed, another's carelessness, can rob people
of their good health. Scientific arrogance accounts for many
more health problems. Our own greed, excesses and passions can cause our own ill health.

These are the things we need healing of!

There is a multitude of possible causes of ill-health, but
for decades, doctors have sought to remedy the symptoms
without exploring the causes. Ideas are changing. The medical world is beginning to acknowledge the effects the mind
can have on the physical health of the body.

An eminent doctor at a medical conference started his lec-
ture by reading a very explicit sexual description. He then
challenged his audience to deny that the mind can have an
effect on the physiology of the body. They couldn't!

There is also the true story of a man dying of cancer in an
American hospital. He was given only two weeks to live, so
he discharged himself and booked into a comfortable hotel.

There, he hired videos of all the funny films he could remember ever having seen, and settled down to watch them. He laughed and laughed his way through them all and, in the end, he was found to be cured!

Disease, sin, suffering and depression are often inter-linked, resulting in many complexities and consequences. Only God knows the whole person. A mind at peace with God and with his people nurtures physical good health. Just to know God is to be healed of many things.

Maybe if we came to know and love God, and through his Son, Jesus Christ, learnt to love and cherish both ourselves and others for his sake, we would be healed of many more ills than we can at present imagine. As we love others, we are also healing them.

To try to understand the mystery of healing, we must look closely at Christ and the people he healed:

● Jairus, a Jew, '... threw himself down at Jesus' feet and begged him to go to his home, because his only daughter ... was dying' (Luke 8:41-42).

Such abandoned prayer! Such incredible expectation of Jesus! Such an act of faith!

Imagine Jairus leaving his dying child, so certain in his own mind that if he could only persuade Jesus to go to his house, all would be well. As it was, Jesus didn't let him down. He never will!

Do we pray for healing with such faith? Stick our necks out and risk looking silly, which Jairus certainly did, as he asked for the seemingly impossible?

● Another official, this time a Roman in Capernaum, who wanted his servant healed, begged Jesus for help but felt too unworthy to have Jesus call at his house (Matthew 8:5-13; Luke 7:1-10). But he was a man who understood authority and he saw Jesus as being one in authority over creation.

Do we *really* believe in Christ's power to alter the process of a sickness? Or do we water that down to his maybe being able to accelerate the natural healing process a little?

Don't ever forget that this is the man who stood up and commanded the wind and the waves! This is the authority that the perceptive Roman officer saw in him.

And listen to Jesus' next statement: '... what you believe will be done for you.' Think of the implication of that!

'And the officer's servant was healed *that very moment*' (Matthew 8:13; emphasis mine).

This surely illustrates Jesus' authority working in harness with a man who had faith and love. God's power has not diminished over these two thousand years. But does our disposition match that of the Roman soldier?

● John tells us about the man born blind, whose 'blindness has nothing to do with his sins or his parents' sins'. This disability is in some way special – 'He is blind so that God's power might be seen at work in him' (9:3).

So sometimes our problems are for God's special use? God wants his power to be made visible in certain situations? He wants it witnessed by others?

We do not ask then, for quiet little miracles that we keep shyly to ourselves – we risk going public! God's healing power must be advertised to all who will listen to the witnessing. Is this one reason why God answers prayers for healing?

● When we look, we see that most of Jesus' healings were done before large groups of people: 'Large crowds came to him, bringing with them the lame, the blind, the crippled, the dumb, and many other sick people, whom they placed at Jesus' feet; and he healed them' (Matthew 15:30). We too must place our sick at Jesus' feet and believe that he will heal them in accordance with his will.

● But healing can bring fear to a crowd too – as when Mob was cured of the evil spirits within him, and the people begged Jesus to go away out of their territory! (Mark 5:1-20).

Does that kind of fear enter our thoughts on healing?

The man himself wanted to follow Jesus, but he told him to 'go back home to your family and tell them how much the Lord has done for you and how kind he has been to you' (Mark 5:19).

How we all need to do this, but how seldom we hear it done or do it ourselves! Are we afraid to?

● Hoping to keep both her problem and the cure to herself, the woman with the issue of blood, shy and self-conscious, thought to herself, 'If I just touch his clothes, I will get well', and 'Jesus knew that power had gone out of him' (Mark 5:28,29).

So her faith drew the Father's power through Jesus, without his consciously directing it towards her!

Might God use us to heal in the same way, directing his power through us, if we make ourselves available? If we go to the place where he wants us to be? If we are totally pliable in his hands, as Jesus was?

'Courage, my daughter! Your faith has made you well' (Matthew 9:22). And a whole crowd of people, from that day through to this, learnt of God's power through her secret troubles! She only touched his cloak and was healed. We can touch him daily in the Eucharist, in prayer and through those we serve.

Many others touched his cloak and all who did, were made well. *All*, not just a few! God's power is still available for all. His touch is still healing people.

● The two blind men (Matthew 9:27-31) were noisier in their approach to Jesus, shouting out, 'Take pity on us, Son of David!' And Jesus called back, 'Do you believe that I can heal you?'

He asks the very same question of us today! And whatever our response to him is, he will repeat what he

68

said to those two men, 'Let it happen, then, just as you believe!'

Healing, in one respect, is in our own hands and hearts! My God, what opportunities we miss!

● Peter did believe in Jesus' power and asked, with complete trust, that he would heal his mother-in-law. Jesus did, of course, heal her. He took her by the hand and helped her up.

Those who care for the sick can do nothing better than ask the Lord to take their loved ones by the hand and lift them up. How he does this is his choice. He may wish to lift them up to heaven – and who are we to argue with that?

In this case, Jesus chose to cure her fever. She, in return, got up and served him, as the crippled woman he healed straightened herself up and praised him (Luke 13:13).

This must surely follow any healing – that God is praised and served as never before! If God wants no more service from us, then we will not be physically healed, but taken to himself, our life's ambition achieved. That's success!

● When we come to look at the miracle of Lazarus being raised to life after being dead for at least four days, we come to the greatest miracle of them all, and the greatest puzzle!

Jesus did not respond immediately to the call of Martha and Mary, but when he did eventually go, he performed a miracle far greater than they would have dared to contemplate. He did have to be asked first, and he did demand Martha's expression of her implicit faith.

We too must ask, and sometimes the answer will not come as and when we want it. But prayer in faith, through Jesus Christ, will most certainly be answered by God in his own time and his own way. It will be more than we dared to ask for and, indeed, may be more than we bargained for!

Jesus asked for Mary to be present before he raised Lazarus. Was that because he wanted her to witness this dramatically powerful act? Was it to prepare her for his own

69

Resurrection, so that she would know from experience that it was perfectly possible? Is he teaching us the same thing?

Did Jesus want Mary to come because he knew that she would attract a large crowd to come with her? Or maybe he knew that Lazarus would need her? What indeed were Lazarus' feelings about being brought back, both then and later, when he caused such a furore amongst the Jews? Had he glimpsed heaven and then had to leave it all behind? And why did Jesus cry? He knew what he was about to do. Was he weeping for other things?

Many of the crowd came to believe in Jesus through this miracle of restoring life. It proved his power over life and death.

Jesus restores life to us all. We have his promise of eternal life. We know he has that power.

● It can have been no less of a marvel for the leper who was healed by the touch of the Lord (Matthew 8:2, 3). This man challenged Jesus quite abruptly: 'Sir, if you want to, you can make me clean'. Christ's simple and loving answer was 'I do want to'. He is as keen and eager to heal us today as he was longing to cleanse the leper. Christ is eager to heal!

● Jesus seemed to like a quick-witted exchange, and he probably still does. The Canaanite woman would not be turned away. In her humility she likened herself to a dog and argued – 'even the dogs under the table eat the children's leftovers!' (Mark 7: 28).

Jesus couldn't resist the combination of persistence, argument, humility, love and faith, and we can be certain that he still finds these qualities irresistible. God is unchanging.

● Often Jesus was implored to heal on behalf of another: '... all who had friends who were sick with various diseases brought them to Jesus; he placed his hands on every one of them and healed them all' (Luke 4:40).

Do we invariably take our friends to Jesus for healing?

Perhaps some of us can derive comfort from the tentativeness of the father who implored: 'Have pity on us and help us, if you possibly can' (Mark 9:22-24). Jesus reflected the wobble in the request. 'Yes, if you yourself can! everything is possible for the person who has faith.' Then the cry came from the heart of the father – 'I do have faith, but not enough. Help me to have more!'

That prayer is so much my own!

● Bartimaeus wasn't tentative. 'Jesus! Son of David! Take pity on me!' (Luke 18:38, 41, 42). 'What do you want me to do for you?' Jesus calls back. 'I want to see again', he said simply. 'Then see! Your faith has made you well.'

Don't we all need healing of some form of blindness? Once healed, we, like Bartimaeus, must follow Jesus, giving thanks and praise to God.

When the crowd saw Bartimaeus, they all praised God! Maybe if our eyes were really opened, we too would inspire a crowd to follow Jesus, giving him praise!

As we intercede for the healing of ourselves or others, Jesus may well be asking us questions as direct as the one he asked Bartimaeus:

'Exactly what do you want me to heal?' Can we be as clear and concise as Bartimaeus?

'What do you really need to be healed of?' Are we only interested in physical healing, whereas God gives priority to the healing of sins? Lord, give us the wisdom to ask for the healing of our habitual sins. There is no point in asking for physical or mental healing, only to resume a sinful life! '... stop sinning or something worse may happen to you' (John 5:14).

'What are your reasons for wanting healing?' Could our request reveal a lack of interest in God's Kingdom, or a lack of trust

in his promise? When death has no fears, the desperation goes out of our desire for healing, and that alone nurtures good health. Certainly, we could daily ask for healing of body, mind and soul, sufficient to be able to do God's will throughout that day. That is the only valid reason for being healed. But God knows our motivation and can't be cheated.

'For whose sake are you asking?' Could there be great selfishness in our request? No use imposing a cure on someone eager to meet the Lord! The prayers of all must be in harmony.

'What is the wisdom of your request?' If we don't trust our own wisdom, we can certainly rely on God's. 'Thy will be done.' Do we pray first to discern the will of God in the situation? Is the Holy Spirit invited into our prayers?

'Are you able to face the consequences of healing?' There could be notoriety or some other hardship. To be healed is to be changed. The blind man can now see! A new life begins in the worship and service of God.

Physical healing is not always right. God may need to use our suffering in some other way. Nor can we demand miracles like some clever magic show.

'"Teacher," they said, "we want to see you perform a miracle," and Jesus replied "No! How evil and godless are the people of this day!"' (Matthew 12:38-39). God does not do tricks! And even Jesus found that his healing power could be blocked by lack of faith.

'He was not able to perform any miracles there ... because the people did not have faith' (Mark 6:5). Jesus was 'greatly surprised' at this. He really expected those who knew him to have faith in his ability to call on his Father's power.

Without faith in him, we cannot draw on God's power. With faith in him, our only limit is the will of God, and we have already seen that he likes us to be whole. Miracles do happen, but they are God-instigated for some unworldly reason, including his glory and his great plan for us.

Sometimes our prayers for healing seem to go unanswered, but God is not deaf, nor hard, nor wrong. He will have his reasons and we must examine ours.

So we come to discover a certain pattern to healing. Because of the intensity of his aching love for us, Jesus wants to be involved in our cleansing and healing. He gives priority to the healing of our sins. We need to be healed of our sins in order to be of full use to God.

On our part, we do have to ask. God has the power to heal in response, provided:

– we have implicit faith in him;

– we repent and turn from our sins;

– we are aware of our own unworthiness (unworthiness doesn't block God's healing, lack of awareness does!);

– we are persistent '... keep on asking' (Luke 11:8);

– we acclaim God's power, so that glory is given to God;

– we go and do God's will – loving, serving, praising.

All healing through Jesus Christ is a declaration of his Messiahship. This was his proof to John the Baptist: '... the blind can see, the lame can walk, those who suffer from dreaded skin-diseases are made clean, the deaf can hear, the dead are raised to life, and the Good News is preached to the poor. How happy are those who have no doubts about me!' (Luke 7:22-23).

Healing and teaching went hand-in-hand throughout Jesus' work on earth. Why is the same emphasis not put on healing today? Have we transferred all our faith to science?

Yet Jesus suggests that we all should heal. 'Go and preach, "The kingdom of heaven is near!" Heal the sick, bring the dead back to life, heal those who suffer from dreaded skin-diseases, and drive out demons' (Matthew 10:7-8).

' .. whoever believes in me will do what I do.' (John 14:12).

'I will do whatever you ask for in my name, so that the Father's glory will be shown through the Son' (John 14:13).

This is a promise for *now* and into the future, not something exhausted two thousand years ago.

'If you ask me for anything in my name, I will do it' (John 14:14).

So many promises that we fail to believe in!

'Believers will be given the power to perform miracles, they will drive out demons in my name; they will speak in strange tongues; ... they will place their hands on sick people, who will get well (Mark 16:17-18).'

Should we claim this power for those we love? There is such a need for discernment, and for this there is a great advantage in belonging to a praying community, whose joint prayers and wisdom will come closer to discerning God's will.

Peter claimed that healing power. He cured the lame man '... in the name of Jesus Christ' (Acts 3:6). Peter had no money, but he gave the beggar what he had – the ability to call on the power of Jesus to heal.

We carry Christ with us. When we are asked for help by anyone, is that what we share with them? Do we offer his power together with our own physical help? How do we come to know if we are meant to be instruments of God's healing?

Jesus loved intensely all those people whom he healed, and we too must sincerely love those for whom we ask healing. In loving them and being open to their needs, we are already on the healing team that God uses.

To sit with them; to listen in a way that allows them to share their fears, their visions, their anxieties, their memories and the reality of their present suffering – all this is healing. To be there, and to help them to be aware that Christ is listening too, is shared prayer at its best. They too come to know that Christ will hear their call – 'Lord, have mercy on us!'

To pray with them, and know that it is God's power that we invoke. To share our implicit faith in that power, believing '... there is nothing that God cannot do' (Luke 1:37).

Being utterly humble before that power, emptying ourselves to be filled with his Spirit. This will bring whatever healing God most desires.

To hold the suffering one close and know that Christ touches them through us. We are his hands and his feet, and if we allow it, he will work through them. We are not alone.

If we are ministers of the Church, we bring the touch of Christ most vividly in the Eucharist and through the Sacrament of the Sick, with the whole Church supporting us in prayer. This is the Lord visiting personally in spite of our unworthiness.

If we are in the medical profession, we bring God's wisdom into our decisions, into our touch, into our choice of treatment. When Christ is in our diagnosis, we are seeing the whole person.

Through the many small, practical services we give to the sick, we bring Jesus' hands to touch the one we serve. Touch seemed so important as he moved among the sick. As we become intensely aware of his presence and his will, each word is his too.

But most of all, Jesus wanted the sick to know and claim God's Kingdom. Through his redeeming act, we are heirs to that Kingdom and we owe it to the sick to share that knowledge, to bring his Word to those who long to hear it. We could be unaware of that longing if we don't broach the subject.

Eventually, we'll come to pray at all times in the presence of our sick – silently, as we listen, as we caress, as we wash them, as we watch by their side, sometimes through the stillness of the night.

Draw Jesus into every action we make, every word we speak, every joke we crack, every smile we share. We *are* part of his healing team. Of course we are meant to be his instruments!

But physical healing is not always appropriate. There is a time to die. God's call will come to each one of us, and we, like Peter, James, Matthew and all God's responsive servants, must drop everything and follow him eagerly. God will not have made a mistake. '... the Lord knows how to rescue godly people from their trials' (2 Peter 2:9).

It is when we are dying that we have our greatest need of healing. No longer physical, but often mental (healing of memories), and always spiritual. To be healed this way leads us to a happy death. In answer to our own prayers and those of others, we could be being healed right to our very last breath on earth. Please God, we will be.

Then God will set our whole being free! Ponder a while on what this could mean for you or a loved one: freedom from pain, worry, phobias, sorrow, disfigurement, freedom of movement, freedom to be our true selves, to love and be loved, freedom from inhibitions, lack of perception, lack of understanding, and all the other lacks. Most of all, healing of our lack of faith!

We will be made utterly whole. That really is healing! We are not meant to last on earth for ever – imperfect people in an imperfect world. Why should we want to? Heaven is ours!

What is important is to live life as richly as possible now, and any life-threatening experiences can certainly intensify that present moment. That too is a gift.

'Don't be afraid, only believe' (Mark 5:36).

7

CARING FOR THE DYING

'I was sick and you took care of me' (Matthew 25:36).

Service

Whether we willingly accept this work or, like Simon of Cyrene, have it thrust upon us, we can find ourselves in many different circumstances, and caught up in many different relationships. Anything from a one-off night sitting with a dying stranger, to years of constant care of someone extremely close to us.

We may be highly qualified in the medical profession, or novice volunteers. Those we care for may be incredibly old or painfully young, each with special needs. We may be caring for them in our own home, a hospice, nursing home or a hospital. Some will be ardent Christians, others not. Some will be seemingly unconscious, others coherent to their last breath.

Whatever the circumstances, when we move to the side of the dying, we become one of a team of people who are there to give physical help, emotional support and spiritual comfort to the one who is dying and to each other. Because we are Christians, we are there in the role of God's servant.

It is difficult, sensitive and exhausting work. But we do not work alone. God is the principal member of the team.

Christ is with the dying, within and beside them. If we serve them, we serve him in a very intimate way, and we are exactly where he is.

Above the baths in Mother Teresa's home in Calcutta, where the sores of the dying are bathed, there is a notice. It reads – THIS IS THE BODY OF CHRIST.

If we can see that reality in the one for whom we care, there is no task too menial, no mess too repulsive, no dressing too repugnant for us. This is serving the Lord in his need. This is healing the indignity of the person we serve. There is a great opportunity in the sick room to serve with love, tenderness and joy. Almighty God, please bless our hands as they touch your Body!

'"I am the Lord's servant", said Mary' (Luke 1:38), a prayer and attitude we can try to emulate. Her servanthood changed the course of her life – and ours! Our acceptance of servanthood will change our lives too – and maybe those of the ones we care for.

'If one of you wants to be great, he must be the servant of the rest; and if one of you wants to be first, he must be the slave of all. For even the Son of Man ... came to serve' (Mark 10:43-45).

Jesus Christ himself said: 'I am among you as one who serves' (Luke 22:27). Almost his last act, as he prepared for his own death, was to serve his friends by way of a most menial task: 'I, your Lord and Teacher, have just washed your feet' (John 13:14). 'If I do not wash your feet, you will no longer be my disciple' (John 13:8).

So, as we work, we have first to allow Jesus to wash our feet. This is his sign to us of how pleased he is that we are there. I have to allow him to cleanse me.

Having accepted his service, we can turn to others and serve them in the same wholehearted, loving way, regardless of how difficult they may be. How deserving we are has never been a condition of Christ's service to us. We can care for the most cantankerous if we remember how God loves and serves them. '... let love make you serve one another. For the whole Law is summed up in one commandment: "Love your neighbour as you love yourself"' (Galatians 5:13-14). 'Help to carry one another's burdens, and in this way you will obey the law of Christ' (Galatians 6:2).

What a wonderful opportunity we have to respond to the Word of God as we work for the sick and the dying!

'You, then, should wash one another's feet' (John 13:14).

One another's. No one does all the washing. We are not meant to struggle alone. Independence is no great virtue. Interdependence in the light of God's love is living Christianity.

So we must allow others to serve us. In this situation, this means we should try to accept all offers of help in our task of caring for the dying, or else we are depriving helpers of their opportunity to serve Christ.

The sick themselves may have ways of serving us, and their service is to be encouraged and warmly accepted. Just their appreciation is very helpful.

We, in our turn, when we come to be dying, will appreciate the cost of such service. But we can draw comfort from knowing that our carers are serving Christ through us. We can help them to realise what they are really doing. We can help them in turn to accept help from all quarters, thus enabling more people to serve the Lord.

As we serve at the bedside of the sick, if we are working with Christ, we will be learning a great deal that will stand us in good stead!

'He helps us in all our troubles, so that we are able to help others who have all kinds of troubles, using the same help that we ourselves have received from God' (2 Corinthians 1:4).

Even God's help is to be shared. We receive nothing to hog to ourselves alone, including our opportunities to serve.

Are we even meant to share our experience of death? It would seem so, but aren't we afraid to do this in our modern secular society? The dying are sedated, secluded and isolated. The dead are sanitised. We fear them. We do not want to know. We expect others, the professionals, to cope with death.

But the Gospel pours out messages to the contrary: '... if anyone does not take care of his relatives, especially the members of his own family, he has denied the faith and is worse than an unbeliever' (1 Timothy 5:8). That is a clear directive, as is: 'Do all your work in love' (1 Corinthians 16:14), and also: 'If you have love for one another, then everyone will know that you are my disciples' (John 13:35).

'... do it with a sincere heart, as though you were serving Christ ... with all your heart do what God wants, as slaves of Christ. Do your work as slaves cheerfully, as though you served the Lord, and not merely men' (Ephesians 6:5-7). And, undeniably, in certain circumstances, care of the terminally ill can feel like slavery! But the guidance continues: 'Be always humble, gentle and patient. Show your love by being tolerant with one another. Do your best to preserve the unity which the Spirit gives by means of the peace that binds you together' (Ephesians 4:2-3).

Truth

This binding together in the Spirit also involves being truthful with each other. No spiritual work can be done through lying and pretending. Those who say, 'Don't let him know that he is dying', are, in my opinion, misguided. There is no kindness in denying the truth at this eleventh hour of life. Gentle prayerfulness will surround that moment of truth. The one who suspects that death is near deserves at least the courtesy of our acknowledging the possibility.

The dying have urgent needs: maybe to prepare themselves emotionally; maybe they want spiritual support from a priest or others; perhaps they long to talk over their fears and doubts; perhaps they need to make their peace with someone; perhaps they want practical help with letter-writing or a debt to be paid, or with putting their affairs in order; maybe they want to draw on our faith to reinforce theirs; maybe they need help to pray.

None of this work can be done if all concerned are masking the truth. Close carers are the ones who often decide for the patient that they would not want to know that they are terminally ill, when all the time it is they themselves who cannot face the hard truth.

It gives me great sorrow to watch a married couple, who all their lives have been honest and open with each other, coming to their last few weeks together and living this lie of pretence – 'No! Of course you're not dying, darling!'

They keep up this façade right to the end sometimes, 'protecting' each other from the truth, while all the time they risk compounding the hurt within, and deny each other the mutual help they both need.

The medical profession too, with its own difficulties in facing death, often connives in this denial of truth, apparently believing that to acknowledge that death is near is to remove all hope.

On the contrary! As I now see it, terminal illness is not a time for battling and resisting death, but a God-given period to learn the final lesson of yielding to the will of God. A time to help each other to come to the point of acceptance and move on to an experience of hope and anticipation. This does *not* mean giving up on life or allowing the quality of life to diminish one jot.

It may be God's will that our loved one is healed. It may not. But God doesn't make mistakes. His timing is perfect. Acceptance brings us to an understanding of this fact and teaches us to trust in God, living our final weeks in harmony with him and with each other.

The dying need our help to focus their eyes on God. To transfer their attention from us to him. What does he want? Your will, Lord, not ours. This way, each is giving the other permission to let go our emotional ties when the time is right.

There is both peace and creativity in living out the will of God. We must help each other to experience this, praying together, crying together if necessary, at all times caring tenderly for the emotional and spiritual needs of each other.

We particularly need to pray before sharing the knowledge of impending death with those we love and are responsible for. Indeed, we can only be certain how to choose our words if we have previously talked together round the subject. And the Holy Spirit will be there to guide us if asked. '... be filled with courage and ... drawn together in love' (Colossians 2:2).

'If you loved me, you would be glad that I am going to the Father' (John 14:28), Jesus said to his disciples. Can we come to have such love as this?

Practical considerations

This area is where we will get the most help from the professionals. If we are nursing our loved ones at home we will be shown how to cope with equipment; how to move the patient as easily as possible; we will be told about medicines, pain relief and diets, and what agencies to contact for nursing help.

But some of the jobs we will be asked to do could be embarrassingly intimate. I have found it helps me to concentrate on trying to preserve the dignity of the sufferer throughout, and a sense of humour is invaluable!

It also helps constantly to remind ourselves that this sick person for whom we are caring is indeed a temple of the Holy Spirit, and so is due every possible care, concern and respect. However unconscious of their own condition they may be, they are entitled to be kept clean and comfortable and even adorned – with hair washed, nails cut and cleaned, and a pretty nightdress, for example. All these jobs are a privilege to do. We can be praying continuously as we go about this work.

Where the dying are preparing for death, there is holy ground, because the Lord is present. We are blessed to be there. We can give him praise by keeping the room sweet-smelling and as attractive as possible. Fresh air, pleasant surroundings and maybe very soft, gentle music will help to make the room a more relaxed place for all concerned.

Mary anointed Jesus for his burial with pure sweet nard. I expect that our Lord smelt of this wherever he appeared after his Resurrection.

We too, in many simple ways, are anointing those we care

for as we wash them and powder them and lovingly make them sweet-smelling. Fragrant gifts for the sick-room seem particularly appropriate – flowers, pot-pourri, soap, talc, and the essential oils that are associated with aromatherapy.

If you are the one taking over all responsibility for the sick person, then it will pay you to accept every possible offer of help, so that you do not become too exhausted as time passes. Then you can be more relaxed in the sick-room, with time to dawdle there.

It makes it easier to sit beside our loved one if we have some simple task to occupy our hands, like embroidery, knitting or sketching. This can encourage easy intermittent talk, and takes away the sense a patient can have that they are wasting our time. Or they can feel that we are watching them too intensely.

They too may still be able to enjoy some craft or hobby, or pass the time contentedly with jigsaw puzzles, crosswords and the like, that can be shared activity, though the duration of their concentration is probably limited. But whatever it is, it pays to find something light-hearted and easy. The intense moments will then be easier to cope with for all those concerned.

Emotional support

There can be a great deal of emotional suffering surrounding terminal illness. Sometimes it is those less closely related to the people concerned who can give the strongest support. They can be there to absorb some of the emotional overspill. They can listen to all the fears expressed, without denying the reality of those fears. They can make allowances for outrageous statements and frayed tempers. If they are implicitly trusted, they may become a sounding-board as relationships are explored in attempts to heal rifts.

It is important that the terminally ill have the opportunity to forgive the wrongs that others have done them. This can take some complicated manoeuvring on the part of the carer to create the opportunity and be out of the way! Here we are working in the realms of very deep feelings and only those who are prepared to become involved in another's suffering are able to help. Neither advice nor judgment is wanted, but rather the ability to understand how that person feels in the depth of anger, or guilt, or fear, or despair.

When we are in this kind of pain, it is reassuring to be both understood and accepted by another human being. It is through this kind of loving acceptance that the unconditional love of God is perceived. This not only gives much-needed support at the time of sharing these feelings, but it enables the sufferer eventually to climb out of the depths. We gain such empathy by listening intently to what the suffering are saying, and maybe even having to struggle to understand what they are *not* saying.

To all this, we bring Christ to listen.

Sometimes, all we can do is hold them close and stay with them as long as they need to be held. We can also give them the consolation of knowing that they are constantly held in our prayers.

This way, we are helping the dying, and those close to them, to face the pains of parting. It doesn't remove the suffering. It does help to make it bearable and maybe understandable. We all come to make sense of things through struggling to express our confusion.

The dying have strong emotional needs. Often they long to be healed of emotional hurts from long, long ago. They will talk of these things, often for the first time ever. We must listen, and not block off their talk with soothing platitudes. It is only ourselves that we comfort this way. They, in fact, are wanting to talk, and are acutely aware of their limited opportunities.

Be demonstrably tender and affectionate with the one who is dying, though I know from experience that it takes a strange amount of courage to break through established barriers of reserve. This can be particularly so with our own parents, who at this stage, are suffering acutely from role reversal. But, 'do not be afraid' (Acts 23:11). Loving touch can melt more formidable barriers than these.

'Let us be concerned for one another, to help one another to show love and to do good' (Hebrews 10:24). And some people do need helpful suggestions as to how they might show their love – so bottled up have their emotions been all their lives.

So dying people can find themselves experiencing the warmth of shared love for the very first time in their lives. We too can discover, almost too late, what a well of love has been dammed up within another.

The dying also have a unique opportunity to be merciful, but again, they may need encouragement and assistance to take that opportunity.

They need the confidence to know that they are unconditionally loved and treasured, particularly as they begin to move away from us to face the overwhelming love of God. And we, who love them, also have a great need to express that love before they leave.

So we come to love, laugh and cry with the dying, more intensely than ever before. Yes, it will be exhausting. So what? We are helping to carry their cross to the end. Don't waste the opportunities, because today's chance doesn't come again tomorrow.

Spiritual comfort
We cannot gauge the spiritual needs of a stranger. We can only ask the Holy Spirit to choose our every word for us. What we can do, is make a simple statement about our own faith, and I have yet to meet someone who is terminally ill, who is entirely uninterested in the idea of eternal life!

Somehow we have to learn to conquer our own resistance to talking about our faith. At this point, time is too short for this selfish reserve. We must find ways of opening up the conversation to explore this gift as far as the patient is willing and able to go. 'Be ready at all times to answer anyone who asks you to explain the hope you have in you, but do it with gentleness and respect' (l Peter 3:15-16).

One person cannot impose belief on another. God himself chooses not to. But we might be so blessed as to be able to make known the love of God. The Holy Spirit will do the rest.

'But how can they call to him for help if they have not believed? And how can they believe if they have not heard the message? And how can they hear if the message is not proclaimed? And how can the message be proclaimed if the messengers are not sent out?' (Romans 10:14-15). (Or if they stay silent when they have gone out?) Lord, make us into messengers with clear voices and life-giving words.

Because we are Christians, when we come close to the dying, we must look for the opportunities to share the Good News:

– we are redeemed
– repent – believe
– accept the promise of eternal life.

'... use ... only helpful words, the kind that build up and provide what is needed, so that what you say will do good to those who hear you' (Ephesians 4:29).

It is a time when we need to be completely dependent upon God. '... the Holy Spirit will teach you at that time what you should say' (Luke 12:12).

As Jesus started his work of bringing his message to the ordinary people, he quoted: 'The Spirit of the Lord is upon me, because he has chosen me to bring good news to the poor. He has sent me to proclaim liberty to the captives and recovery of sight to the blind; to set free the oppressed and announce that the time has come when the Lord will save his people' (Luke 4:18-19).

The Lord has chosen us, who are close to the dying, to do similar work, though in an infinitely more minor role. To avoid that work might be to deprive someone of the chance to come to know and love God in the last few weeks of their life.

It is important, then, that we discover if the one we have come to care for *has* heard the Good News. Do they believe it or want to believe it? Do we have an eagerness, tempered with sensitivity, to share what we have been given as a free gift? And, indeed, when it is our turn to be cared for, have those who cared for us also heard that same message? We could be servants of God right to the end.

Sadly, it is not always possible to share this precious message. This is extremely painful when it is resisted by those we love dearly. We can then only trust that the intensity of our prayers for them will bring them safely into God's keeping in spite of themselves. His love for them will never waver. Nor must ours. They will reach God through this entanglement in his love.

To be with a committed Christian as death approaches is to be greatly enriched. They are so close to God. They are being changed. As are we. Husband and wife; mother and child; the sick one and the carer – can together focus their attention on Jesus Christ, our Redeemer, and his promise of eternal life.

We need to agree on what we are praying for and we can't know that if we don't talk together. Then we must make time to come together to speak to the Father in the name of Jesus his Son. '... whenever two of you on earth agree about anything you pray for, it will be done for you by my Father in heaven. For where two or three come together in my name, I am there with them' (Matthew 18:19-20).

Such prayers *will* be answered – in God's own way and his choice of time. Trust his choice.

'... be filled with the Spirit. Speak to one another with the words of psalms, hymns and sacred songs; sing hymns and psalms to the Lord with praise in your hearts' (Ephesians 5:18-19). This brings to mind a gentle soul whom I met recently, who always sang her ailing husband to sleep with his favourite hymns. What a peaceful way of praying together.

87

There are so many different ways in which we can help our loved ones to focus their thoughts on the God whom they are approaching. We are required to be creative and sensitive in finding appropriate ways. These simple suggestions are merely to stir the imagination to better ways:

● prayers on the radio; 'Thought for the Day'; the Sunday morning service etc. on the radio and TV;

● a crucifix on the wall might be a focus for their eyes; or perhaps they need to handle it;

● rosary beads, if the sick person has treasured these in their earlier life;

● music from Taizé is spiritual and prayer-evoking;

● a candle, placed safely at a distance, can be symbolic of the light of Christ;

● maybe they can still read easily, in which case have their familiar prayer books, Gospels and Psalms to hand;

● perhaps they could be inspired by the spiritual exercises suggested by Gerard Hughes in his *God of Surprises*;

● some poetry reveals rich spiritual insight and a dying person can be more sensitive to the arts than they have ever been before;

● from time to time, select and read a short extract from the Bible; familiar passages can take on a new meaning at this time of heightened awareness. To dawdle for a few minutes longer to talk over the passage together, may teach us both a great deal. Each situation is unique and God will have his own special message for each one.

These few quotations are merely to help you do your own searching:

1. 'Mary... sat down at the feet of the Lord and *listened* to his teaching' (Luke 10:39; emphasis mine). Take time off to sit together to listen to him. Even at this time of peak stress, avoid being a Martha twenty-four hours a day. The Lord says to us, as he said to her, 'You are worried and troubled over so many things, but just one is needed. Mary has cho-

sen the right thing' (Luke 10: 41-42). If the Lord speaks, stop to listen, even at the most pressurised times.

2. '... like a lamb that makes no sound when its wool is cut off, he did not say a word' (Acts 8:32).

Maybe the sick, facing many indignities, can identify with Jesus as never before. Now they are able to align themselves with Christ crucified. They may want us to stay close and hold them for a while as they express their own vulnerability, their sense of brokenness.

3. '... I live by faith in the Son of God, who loved me and gave his life for me. I refuse to reject the grace of God' (Galatians 2:20-21). Approaching death – an appropriate time to accept wholeheartedly every grace from God. He will be generous to the open-hearted.

4. 'Be like new-born babies, always thirsting for the pure spiritual milk, so that by drinking it you may grow up and be saved'(1 Peter 2:2). Fancy being able to give such a freshness of image to a dying man of eighty! But it applies as much to him as to anyone. He may need someone to bring him the milk!

5. 'How many times have I wanted to put my arms round all your people, just as a hen gathers her chicks under her wings, but you would not let me!' (Matthew 23:37). Those who are sick need to know that they can slip under God's wing at any time. Encourage them to indulge in this comfort rather than resist it.

6. Jesus preached, 'The right time has come and the Kingdom of God is near! Turn away from your sins and believe the Good News!' (Mark 1:15). The Kingdom of God is specially near to the terminally ill. This is to be contemplated with joy, curiosity, awe, excitement and all the other human feelings involved.

Believe that Jesus *has* saved us from God's wrath and disgust. He has purchased our position of friendship. That relationship is to be marvelled at. The imagination is allowed to explore it.

7. Words for both the patient and the nurse: 'Show a gentle attitude towards everyone. The Lord is coming soon. Don't worry about anything, but in all your prayers ask God for what you need, always asking him with a thankful heart. And God's peace, which is far beyond human understanding, will keep your hearts and minds safe in union with Christ Jesus' (Philippians 4:5-7).

This way, death has no fears for either those who go or those who are left. It is not easy. We may have had a good few fights and arguments with the Lord on the way. But when we let go of both ourselves and our loved ones, we come to the will of God and are in union with him.

Ponder these things as Mary did and leave the one we care for, thinking deeply about the Word.

Sometimes the sick can be too ill or too confused to be able to participate in prayer. Then we must assume the responsibility of taking them to Jesus or calling him to them, with the same persistence as the men who lowered their friend through the roof. We have to find a way of getting Jesus to touch them. The anointing in the Sacrament of the Sick is one obvious way.

We must audibly pour out our prayers for the dying even if they seem unconscious. Hearing is the last of the senses to leave us, and if you think about it, even as we sleep normally, we drift in and out of hearing without giving any visible sign of doing so. We have no means of knowing how our prayers and readings may be sinking deep into the mind and heart of the apparently unconscious. The Lord will be listening attentively to both of us.

Even at a time of heavy sedation the Lord will surely be at work within the seemingly passive body, preparing the spirit for its great meeting. We can pray that he is.

'Stay here and keep watch with me' (Matthew 26:38), may be the silent plea of the dying. And the dying person may himself be watching and waiting with our Redeemer, somehow being allowed to share in that redemptive act.

While our patient is conscious we want to give them simple food for thought in the same way that we will be feeding them simple, nourishing food. There will be appropriate times to do this and a right time to leave them alone with their own thoughts. Be guided by the Holy Spirit.

Throughout the work that we are doing, we are attempting to give purpose to the one who is dying:

1. 'God's free gift is eternal life' (Romans 6:23).

Death is the opportunity to accept that gift as eagerly as we accepted the gift of life on earth. Terminal illness is when we can say a heartfelt 'Yes, please', to that gift.

2. God's power moves into our weakness. If we have learnt how to rely on that power in our active lives, it will be there at the time of our greatest weakness:

'I am most happy, then, to be proud of my weaknesses, in order to feel the protection of Christ's power over me ... For when I am weak, then I am strong' (2 Corinthians 12:9-10). So there is strength in death, God's strength.

3. Nobody's suffering is a waste of time. Somehow, it would seem to contribute to the redemption of the world and those who suffer can draw great consolation from this.

4. Their prayers are powerful. They are so close to God. Ask for the help of their prayers for our own work and that of others we care for.

5. The dying teach us about death as no one else can. Make them aware of how they are helping us. When our own time comes, we will realise that the very way we face death will influence those around us to examine their own relationship with the Almighty. We could be instruments of God's love at the very hour of our greatest weakness.

6. But, there can be no greater purpose in our death than that through it, we reach our resurrection. Our new beginning.

Jesus said clearly: 'Your brother will rise to life', and Martha affirmed it: 'I know that he will rise to life on the last day' (John 11:23,24). She had no doubts at all because she had listened to Jesus' teachings and had believed.

91

We too *know* that the one we care for will also be given eternal life, and our whole care of the dying must act out that belief in order to strengthen their faith.

The apostles preached everywhere '... the sacred and ever-living message of eternal salvation' (Mark 16:10). What sweeter thoughts for the dying than their promised new life?

'... our religion, which is based on the hope for eternal life. God, who does not lie, promised us this life before the beginning of time' (Titus 1:2).

Jesus said: 'It is better for you to enter life without a hand or a foot...' (Matthew 18:8). Enter life – this is how Jesus described death!

✻ ✻ ✻

Those who assist the dying can themselves be screaming in agony at the pain of separation, or they can be working with God in the process of dying – like a midwife working to ease the pain, trying to assist this entry into a new life, making it all as smooth as possible, seeing terminal illness as being like a pregnancy for eternal life.

This is the great letting go – our greatest and final gift to our beloved – that we release them trustingly and gratefully into the hands of the Lord.

They will be made whole in death. Alleluia!

'Where, Death, is your victory? Where, Death, is your power to hurt?' (1 Corinthians 15:55).

Sudden death

This poses different problems, particularly for those who are suddenly bereaved. They don't have the opportunities examined above – the privilege of nursing their loved ones, time to talk things over and adjust to new situations, shared prayer, the coming to terms with the letting go process, etc. This causes them an agony of feelings round things left undone and unsaid, all complicated by their being in shock. But when sudden death is due to natural causes, the Lord would seem to command – 'Come now!' We cannot argue.

We do not dawdle. How nice! This would be my choice. But the Gospel is full of warnings to be ready to die:

'Be on your guard, then, because you do not know what day your Lord will come' (Matthew 24:42).

And facing the thought of sudden death with equanimity does surely require some practice in being obedient to the will of God, today. Then we will be ready to respond to him at the drop of a hat. Also it requires that we accept that we belong to God and that he is entitled to take us or our beloved at any time he chooses – as the timing of our birth was his choice. We never question that!

Death '... will come as suddenly as the pains that come upon a woman in labour, ... the Day should not take you by surprise like a thief' (1 Thessalonians 5:3-4).

Like someone fitted with an emergency phone, we should have some expectation of it ringing. We know that one day we will be called. '... the Son of Man will come at an hour when you are not expecting him' (Matthew 24:44). 'Be on your guard, then, because you do not know the day or the hour' (Matthew 25:13).

Indeed, the older we grow, the more reason to be ready, so 'Get rid of all bitterness, passion, and anger... no more hateful feelings of any sort. Instead, be kind and tender-hearted to one another, and forgive one another, as God has forgiven you through Christ' (Ephesians 4:31-32).

This is work to do now, just in case we have an urgent call! And for me – at sixty – I cannot have a really unexpected death from now on.

'Be on watch, be alert, for you do not know when the time will come' (Mark 13:33). We all have an appointed time to die and we cannot evade it even were we to run to the far side of the earth in disguise.

'Be on your guard! Don't let yourselves become occupied with too much feasting and drinking and with the worries of this life, or that Day may suddenly catch you like a trap' (Luke 21:34).

(God Almighty, I still have so much to learn before I am ready. Help me not to panic, because you can teach me so much within a moment, if only I am willing to learn.)

But some sudden deaths are horrific, brought about by a deliberate act of violence or by indifference to the sanctity of life. It must be terrifying to come face to face with naked evil in another human being. It would evoke very powerful emotions including, maybe, a responding violence in ourselves. How terrible to meet the Lord when full of anger!

We have to learn, at all times of stress, to call upon God for help: '... whoever calls out to the Lord for help will be saved' (Acts 2:21). Maybe not saved from disaster, but saved from submitting to the evil.

Then look at this reaction: 'Full of fear, they praised God' (Luke 5:26). Could that ever be our own reaction to fear? To inflicted pain? To being attacked? (I need help with that one Lord – to praise God our Father next time that I'm afraid!)

We are never alone. Whatever we experience, however alarming and unexpected, God is with us and he is not taken by surprise. He is with us most intensely in our fear. People who have survived a disaster will often testify to an acute awareness of the presence of God. God can take the very worst of tragedies and turn them to the advantage of those who trust him. The Crucifixion is the prime example. It is so very hard though, to have God's perspective on our own personal disaster.

It is obvious that those who are blessed with sudden death do not drift gradually towards the Lord, supported by their loved ones. They leap towards him, alone. What a shock if we have never previously contemplated the possibility.

What a shock anyway!

How hard it is to come to terms with sudden bereavement through the smothering blanket of shock and horror which engulfs the one who is left behind, the one who hasn't had a chance to become a carer.

But the Lord always knows best.

8

THE MAJOR ROLE OF PRAYER

Prayer is our own personal communication line open to Almighty God. Through prayer, we change and come to some understanding of the will of God.

Paul prayed '...that Christ will make his home in your hearts through faith. I pray that you may have your roots and foundation in love, so that you, together with all God's people, may have the power to understand how broad and long, how high and deep, is Christ's love. Yes, may you come to know his love – although it can never be fully known – and so be completely filled with the very nature of God. To him who by means of his power working in us is able to do so much more than we can ever ask for, or even think of: to God be the glory in the church and in Christ Jesus for all time, for ever and ever! Amen' (Ephesians 3:17-21).

How enriching if this prayer could be adapted for the whole caring team to pray together. Perhaps this can be done within a Christian hospice, or within one's own home. At least we can pray it with our beloved sick and anyone else who cares to join us. We can leave it written out and placed prominently for anyone to read who dawdles by the bedside.

As we pray, we must believe that our prayers will be answered and our loved ones will indeed become filled with the very nature of God.

And so we serve them – both God and humankind. What a privilege our nursing has become! What spiritual growth we are allowed to share in! What a fantastic and shared experience death could be if we are open to each other, and allow the Spirit to work with us to convert our vision into reality.

Prayers *with* the dying

It seems important that we should set aside a regular time to be together to pray. There might be some shyness about suggesting this, and perhaps some difficulty finding the right format to begin with, but almost certainly it will quickly become the most precious time of the day, from which will spring strength, joy and a richness of understanding. One or more of the following might be helpful to get started:

'In the name of our Lord Jesus Christ, always give thanks for everything to God the Father' (Ephesians 5:20).

For everything! That means that as we pray together, we have to give thanks for our present experience of terminal illness. There will be many blessings that infuse this experience. We are to claim them and give God thanks.

Together, we could create our personal litany of thanksgiving for the blessings received throughout our lives.

'Let us give thanks to the God and Father of our Lord Jesus Christ, the merciful Father, the God from whom all help comes!' (2 Corinthians 1:3).

Pray together for a strengthening of our faith. Jesus said: 'I am the resurrection and the life. Whoever believes in me will live, even though he dies; and whoever lives and believes in me will never die' (John 11:25-26).

Here, Jesus gives us a clear statement and follows it with a straight question: 'Do you believe this?' (John 11:26).

Our praying together will help each of us to believe. Indeed, the gift of unshakeable faith is the most perfect answer to all our prayers.

Jesus also said: 'I am the way, the truth, and the life; no one goes to the Father except by me' (John 14:6). A relationship with him is essential. He promises to resurrect us: 'I will come back and take you to myself, so that you will be where I am' (John 14:3).

That can only be heaven. Have no doubts about this, and no anxieties about the destiny of the one who is dying. 'Do not be worried and upset; do not be afraid' (John 14:27).

When we are dying, the sacramental Church is at its supportive best, pouring out the grace of God upon us. Bring in the Church to administer the Sacrament of the Sick. Invite in the minister who can best help the one who is sick to experience repentance.

Christ likens himself to the good shepherd who '... goes looking for the one that got lost until he finds it. When he finds it, he is so happy that he puts it on his shoulders and carries it back home' (Luke 15:4-6). Console the dying with this when they feel sinful and unworthy. Call out to the Shepherd so that he will find our loved one. Together, contemplate the fact that '... there will be more joy in heaven over one sinner who repents than over ninety-nine respectable people who do not need to repent' (Luke 15:7).

Just think, by accepting our sinfulness and being genuinely sorry for any offence we have given our God, we make him so happy that he wants to celebrate with all the heavenly company! Such is the extreme of his love for us. Such is the welcome awaiting us sinners!

Believe it! Trust it! And imagine the celebrations!

Urge the Church to share the Eucharist regularly with our sick. This way they become, more intensely, a part of the Body of Christ.

'And the bread we break: when we eat it, we are sharing in the body of Christ... (and) all of us, though many, are one body, for we all share the same loaf' (1 Corinthians 10:16-17).

'So let us come near to God with a sincere heart and a sure faith, with hearts that have been purified from a guilty conscience and with bodies washed with clean water. Let us hold on firmly to the hope we profess, because we can trust God to keep his promise' (Hebrews 10:22-23). *Not* to believe that we are safe in death, is to call God a liar!

Pray together for strength, '... be strong through the grace that is ours in union with Christ Jesus'(2 Timothy 2:1).

All of us have our own need for strength and courage at this testing and exhausting time. Pray for each other's needs. Voice them, so that we have a deep understanding between us and know exactly what we are praying for.

'Do not lose your courage, then, because it brings with it a great reward. You need to be patient, in order to do the will of God and receive what he promises. For, as the scripture says,

"Just a little while longer,

and he who is coming will come;

he will not delay.

My righteous people, however, will

believe and live;

but if any of them turns back,

I will not be pleased with him.

We are not people who turn back and are lost. Instead, we have faith and are saved"' (Hebrews 10:35-39).

'Let us keep our eyes fixed on Jesus, on whom our faith depends from beginning to end. He did not give up because of the cross!' (Hebrews 12:2).

Maybe we could spend some of our prayer time together, simply talking over the character of Jesus as we each see him, recalling incidents in the Gospels that reveal his thoughts and feelings, as we might talk over the feelings of a mutual friend – as indeed he is.

Sacred music; hymns; a cross; a candle; rosary beads; an empty begging bowl – these different aids and symbols might help some people to draw even closer to God. Talk about what might be helpful. Make suggestions. We have an opportunity to be imaginative, planning something soothing for those who need to sleep and something more stimulating for those who want to occupy their minds, leaving them to their own thoughts when appropriate. What sensitivity we need! God help us. But remember, the Holy Spirit will be at work with us, presenting rich symbolism in the very shadows of the room.

As those we look after diminish physically, they are touching God's glory. Recall together the meaning of glory:

splendour; heavenly bliss; triumphant honour; beauty; resplendent brightness; summit of attainment or gratification; a burst of sunlight; the presence of God; a representation of the heavens opened; to rejoice (*Chambers Twentieth Century Dictionary*).

Beside this definition, the term *giving glory* to God seems monstrously impertinent. I can only interpret this for myself as trying to appreciate the wonder of God, however inadequately. As I grow closer to God, I grow in appreciation, and so give greater glory to God, though still infinitesimal. But God is pleased, as any parent is delighted with their baby's gurgle of recognition. We can never add anything to the greatness of God but we can please him.

'Lift up your tired hands, then, and strengthen your trembling knees! Keep walking on straight paths' (Hebrews 12:12-13). '... the time has come for you to wake up from your sleep. For the moment when we will be saved is closer now ... the night is nearly over' (Romans 13:11-12).

As the one who is sick weakens, we must try to give them the sense that our prayers are their prayers too, and they can rest within them. At this stage we should still pray aloud, but probably use only familiar prayers and keep them short.

If we start now to gather together appropriately brief prayers, writing them into a simple exercise book, we will be able to read from them at a time when we may be drained of physical and spiritual energy. Prayers such as the following:

'Remember me, Jesus, when you come as King!' (Luke 23:42).

'God bless the King who comes in the name of the Lord! Peace in heaven and glory to God!' (Luke 19:38).

'May God the Father and Christ Jesus our Lord give you grace, mercy, and peace' (1 Timothy 1:2).

'Peace be with you' (Luke 24:36).

Prayers can be copied from books of services that are most treasured and familiar, such as the Daily Missal, or Matins, or the Book of Daily Prayer.

What I term jingle prayers become valuable, as they are short and to the point:

'Lord have mercy on us.' 'Jesus I love You.' 'God be with you.' 'Make me an instrument of your peace.' 'Glory to you, O God.' The Fathers of the Desert termed these 'arrow prayers' – short phrases aimed heavenwards.

The Lord's prayer cannot be said too often.

A short act of contrition will be full of meaning and feeling, and the prayers of the Stations of the Cross, if they are familiar, are particularly appropriate as the one who is sick begins actively to share the passion and death of our Lord, as they never have previously.

The Psalms are the words that Jesus often used to his Father. To echo them is to pray through Christ. They are so rich in mood, that I make no excuse for quoting extensively from them, but for maximum enrichment, each must find their own treasury. To be familiar with them long before death will give us a vocabulary of prayer for all our needs.

Acknowledging our guilt

All of Psalms 37 and 50

To You all flesh will come
with its burden of sin.
Too heavy for us, our offences,
but you wipe them away. (Psalm 64:3,4)

O God, you know my sinful folly;
my sins you can see. (Psalm 68:6)

Asking for forgiveness

Do not remember the sins of my youth.
Lord, for the sake of your name
forgive my guilt, for it is great. (Psalm 24:7,11)

Lord, have mercy on me,
heal my soul for I have sinned against you. (Psalm 40:5)

Redeem us because of your love! (Psalm 43:27)

Asking for guidance

Lord, make me know your ways.
Lord, teach me your paths. (Psalm 24:4)

Bend my heart to your will. (Psalm 118:36)

Make me know the way I should walk:
Teach me to do your will. (Psalm 142:8,10)

Cry of distress

Have mercy on me, Lord, I have no strength;
Lord, heal me, my body is racked;
my soul is racked with pain. (Psalm 6:3,4)

Do not leave me alone in my distress. (Psalm 21:12)

Lord, my God, I call for help by day;
I cry at night before you.
For my soul is filled with evils;
my life is on the brink of the grave. (Psalm 87:2,4)

Do not hide your face from me
in the day of my distress. (Psalm 101:3)

Cry of the suffering servant

My God, my God, why have you forsaken me?
O my God, I call by day and you give no reply;
I call by night and I find no peace. (Psalm 21:2,3)

It is your face, O Lord, that I seek;
hide not your face.
Dismiss not your servant in anger;
Do not abandon or forsake me. (Psalm 26:8,9)

In your compassion, turn towards me. (Psalm 68:17)

Why, O Lord, do you hold back your hand? (Psalm 73:11)

How long must your servant suffer? (Psalm 118:84)

Trust in God

Blessed are they who put their trust in God. (Psalm 2:12)

You may mock the hope of the poor,
but their refuge is the Lord. (Psalm 13:6)

Guard me as the apple of your eye.
Hide me in the shadow of your wings. (Psalm 16:8)

(All of Psalm 22 – The Lord is my shepherd)

Happy those who have placed their trust in the Lord.
(Psalm 39:5)

Thanking God

Give thanks to the Lord, tell his name,
make known his deeds among the peoples. (Psalm 104:1)

O give thanks to the Lord for he is good,
for his great love is without end. (Psalm 135:1)

All of Psalm 137

Praising God

How great is your name, O Lord our God,
through all the earth. (Psalm 8:2)

'I will praise you, Lord, with all my heart;
I will recount all your wonders.
I will rejoice in you and be glad,
and sing psalms to your name, O Most High. (Psalm 9:2,3)

All of Psalm 18

Ring out your joy to the Lord, O you just;
for praise is fitting for loyal hearts. (Psalm 32:1)

Let his glory fill the earth. (Psalm 71:19)

All of Psalms 92 and 150

Expression of faith

God will ransom me from death
and take my soul to himself. (Psalm 48:16)

My help shall come from the Lord
who made heaven and earth. (Psalm 120:2)

Expression of hope

All of Psalm 15

I am sure I shall see the Lord's goodness
in the land of the living.
Hope in him, hold firm and take heart.
Hope in the Lord! (Psalm 26:13,14)

Expression of joy

The Lord is King, let earth rejoice. (Psalm 96 :1)

My soul shall be joyful in the Lord
and rejoice in his salvation. (Psalm 34:9)

This day was made by the Lord;
we rejoice and are glad. (Psalm 117:24)

The song of a happy person

All of Psalm 91

Fear of the Lord

To fear the Lord is the first stage of wisdom;
all who do so prove themselves wise. (Psalm 110:10)

O blessed are you who fear the Lord
and walk in his ways! (Psalm 127:1)

Seeking comfort

Have mercy on me, God, have mercy
for in you my soul has taken refuge.
In the shadow of your wings I take refuge
till the storms of destruction pass by. (Psalm 56:2)

You are close to all who call you,
who call on you from their hearts.
Lord, you protect all who love you. (Psalm 144:18)

God's love for us

The Lord is compassion and love,
slow to anger and rich in mercy. (Psalm 102:8)

O give thanks to the Lord for he is good;
for his love endures forever. (Psalm 106:1)

To ponder the brevity and fragility of life

All of Psalm 89

A beautiful prayer for old age

All of Psalm 70

Planted in the house of the Lord
they will flourish in the courts of our God,
still bearing fruit when they are old,
still full of sap, still green,
to proclaim that the Lord is just. (Psalm 91:14-16)

Asking for release from life on earth

You are my rescuer, my help,
O God, do not delay. (Psalm 39:18)

Like the deer that yearns
for running streams,
so my soul is yearning
for you, my God. (Psalm 41:2)

My heart is ready, O God,
my heart is ready. (Psalm 56:8)

O God, make haste to my rescue,
Lord, come to my aid! (Psalm 69:2)

Lord, make haste and answer;
for my spirit fails within me.
Do not hide your face
lest I become like those in the grave. (Psalm 142:7)

Reach down from heaven and save me. (Psalm 143:7)

When we pray the Psalms, we join the whole communion of saints – and they join us!

Prayers *for* the dying

Gradually, as the one who is dying begins to lose energy and, perhaps, consciousness, we may find that the character of our prayer changes. We can still pray aloud so that sometimes the dying person will be aware of what we are doing for them, and be comforted.

If we remember always to pray that God's will be done, and when asking for help, always ask in the name of the Lord, we are aligning ourselves and our sick with him. Our prayers will be answered. '... the Father will give you whatever you ask him for in my name' (John 16:23). As we ourselves strive to serve God and our sick one, our prayers will be powerful. Love, service, faith and persistence – we have seen that these are irresistible to God!

Even if we feel that the one who is dying has continually resisted the love of God, we must pray with faith. Jesus is the Good Shepherd. He does not want to lose a single lamb.

When we pray for those who have moved away from God, we ask for something that must be completely to God's liking. Our prayers, therefore, must be answered – in God's time and in his way. We must not doubt this.

'Pray in the power of the Holy Spirit, and keep yourselves in the love of God, as you wait for our Lord Jesus Christ in his mercy to give you eternal life' (Jude 20). Us, and our loved ones too.

'Our God is merciful and tender. He will cause the bright dawn of salvation to rise on us and to shine from heaven on all those who live in the dark shadow of death, to guide our steps into the path of peace' (Luke 1:78-79).

What gentle encouragement is there!

'May the God of peace provide you with every good thing

you need in order to do his will' (Hebrews 13:21).

We pray that our loved ones are experiencing this peace and are already responding to his will.

As death grows closer, group prayer can be incredibly supportive to both the dying and ourselves, if it is an experience that we are at ease with.

'They gathered frequently to pray as a group' (Acts 1:14), and '... as a witness to the resurrection of the Lord Jesus' (Acts l:21), as we too must witness to the Risen Lord.

Group prayer should be full of hope and joy to sustain all concerned. And the people within the group need to be sensitive to the household – respecting their privacy.

As Jesus died, the army officer praised God! Will we too be able to do this as our loved one dies? Yes, if we have been hand-in-hand with God throughout the experience.

Prayers *of* the dying

One day, we ourselves will be the ones approaching death. Because of Jesus Christ, we can face that prospect with confidence. '... rest assured in hope, because you will not abandon me in the world of the dead; you will not allow your faithful servant to rot in the grave. You have shown me the paths that lead to life, and your presence will fill me with joy' (Acts 2:26-28).

We have ahead of us a unique experience of standing on the threshold of God's glory, poised to leap into the unknown yet known.

At this time of approaching death, we are to be as children, asking for nothing for ourselves, but expecting constant care and protection from our loving Father, trusting in his generous love.

At long last, we can stop trying to manipulate events to go our way. 'Your Father already knows what you need before you ask him' (Matthew 6:8).

Hold out the begging bowl and accept with gratitude anything he gives us. Even suffering! Accept the Lord's care, understanding and choice of time. Remember, our prayers are powerful at this time. We are so close to God. Christ asks, 'What do you want me to do for you? (Matthew 20:32). Here is our opportunity to turn our attention to others.

When Jesus was tempted by Satan in the desert, he was determined not to use his Father's power for his own good. Is this what we should be like? Not calling on God's power to help ourselves, but using it only for others?

'... before the end comes, the gospel must be preached to all people' (Mark 13:10). If we have insights now, they are to be shared. The dying are listened to with great respect. Their words are remembered with a special intensity and are well deliberated on. (This is better expressed by John of Gaunt in Richard II (II. i. 5): 'The tongues of dying men enforce attention like deep harmony. Where words are scarce, they are seldom spent in vain; for they breathe truth that breathe their words in pain.')

When close to God '... the words you speak will not be yours; they will come from the Holy Spirit' (Mark 13:11).

We can look to how Stephen died, praying for those who persecuted him. We too can release from guilt all those who have hurt us. 'Lord! Do not remember this sin against them! (Acts 7:60)

And we can pray as he prayed, 'Lord Jesus, receive my spirit!' (Acts 7:59). 'Whoever holds out to the end will be saved' (Mark 13:13). 'The end of all things is near. You must be self-controlled and alert, to be able to pray' (1 Peter 4:7).

But, unfortunately, the restless aching pain or the dragging weight of our illness may be hard to penetrate with prayer. Our brains may be muddled with age or pain or drugs. Please God we will be able to rest on the prayers of others, while our own prayers may have to be reduced to the simplest of our well-practised exercises, e.g.

– Prayer in the Name of Jesus: repeating the name of Jesus, holding only that in our minds.

– The breathing prayer – matching the rhythm of our breathing: 'Lord, I breathe you in, and myself out'.

– Stillness: 'Be still and know that I am God' (Psalm 45:11), and perhaps for the first time we are brought to real stillness before God.

● Jingle prayers:
'Lord have mercy!'
'Praise be to God.'
'My Lord and my God!'
'Holy, holy, holy, Lord God Almighty!'
'Lord, the spirit is willing, but the flesh is weak.'

● The 'GLORY' prayer – Dwell on the meaning of God's glory. Believe that we will share it.

● Call to the Lord – 'God richly blesses all who call out to him.' (Romans 10:12)

● *Maranatha*: a mantra for the dying, meaning 'Come, Lord Jesus' (1 Corinthians 16:22).

● Do not be afraid: 'I will never leave you; I will never abandon you' (Hebrews 13:5).

● Sacrifice– each pain, the indignity, the loneliness – all offered to God for his use.

● The cross – Contemplate the value of Christ's cross. Ponder the purpose of our own.

● Imagine – Jesus sitting on the side of the bed. Watch him. Imagine – holding out the begging bowl before the Lord. Say – 'Give me what I need, to do your will today. Heal me of all that might resist your will.'

109

● Imagine – ourselves as a single grain of sand in a huge desert – so insignificant are we. Yet we are known and loved by God. Marvel at it!

● Emptiness– in the emptiness of our desert, wait for God.

● Waiting – 'Be still before the Lord and wait in patience' (Psalm 36:7). To wait, is prayer.
Hopefully, at the moment of death, we will be able to echo Jesus' last prayer: 'Father! Into your hands I commend my spirit' (Psalm 30:6).

Any of these prayers that attract us can become a part of our daily prayer pattern *now*, while we have health of mind and body and the ability to concentrate. This way we are submerging ourselves in Christ. What better way to learn to die?

9

THE EXPERIENCE OF DEATH

I once heard a preaching priest advise his congregation not to be curious about life after death, because we could never know what heaven would be like.

No, we can't *know*, but surely we can let our imaginations play round the many clues that Christ was keen to give us!

Perhaps, by projecting ourselves imaginatively into any anticipated experience, we find a way of exploring some of the aspects of that experience. Then when we come to it in reality, we are already responsive and receptive. In this mood, I explore the process of returning to God via death. Of course it is a very personal view, and is therefore very limited.

I believe that we have been in the mind of the Creator since before time began. Our proper place is with him. That is where we belong. It is as if we have already existed with him, but have slipped away from him to live on earth for a short time, to work with him on his creation.

We will be drawn back to him at the end of that allowed working time. We shall be known and recognised in heaven, and it will all seem familiar to us. Even here on earth,we can long for that which we once had, though the memory is a mere spider's thread.

Life on earth, then, is our God-given opportunity to work with him in the effort and hassle of creation.

Death marks the end of these opportunities. (Horrifyingly, my life could be a whole load of missed opportunities because I haven't realised my true function!) Death is simply the method of returning to God.

Letting go of life
Years ago I heard this story on the radio (I wish I could attribute it to the right author). A little boy asked his grand-

mother what it would be like to die. She said it could be either easy or hard, and then she illustrated to the little boy what she meant.

She put him in a chair with wooden arms, and told him to cling on tightly. Then she wrestled with him, pulling and tugging to get him free, until a final wrench got him out – hot, towsled and not a little bruised.

Then she told him to climb back into the chair. 'This time', she said, 'put your arms round my neck.' As he did so, she lifted him easily out of the chair. Death, she suggested, could be either of those experiences.

Like the people to whom the king sent his son with invitations to the feast (Matthew 22:1-14), do we refuse God's invitation to his Kingdom, kicking, screaming, fighting and resisting him to the very end?

'Father, the hour has come' (John 17:1). This was Jesus' prayer of turning full face towards his Father, acknowledging and accepting the start of his death journey.

There comes an hour in terminal illness when we too must turn to the Almighty with outstretched arms. This is the hour of hearing God's call – 'Follow Me.'

To the sensitive observer, that point in time is often marked by some sense of change – a time of special clarity; a certain kind of stillness; a sense of saying a special goodbye; a feeling of emptiness; or maybe an experience of darkness; a vacuum.

I see this as the starting-point from which the soul begins its journey towards God – as on one particular day, a child lies still in its mother's womb, poised ready for birth.

The Holy Spirit will move into that stillness and wait with us, teaching us all the while. '... the Holy Spirit ... will teach you everything and make you remember all that I have told you' (John 14:26).

I suspect we will do a lot of remembering and discovering as we wait – a necessary preparation for what is to come. Amongst other things, we will be remembering and discovering that we have no need to be afraid!

People who have had some sort of out-of-body experience when they have been close to death, speak of a great sense of peace, well-being and light. They seldom have any desire to return to the restrictions of their bodies. Death, for some, would seem to be a beautiful experience. But even if death is more like a storm, we know that Christ urges us to have faith, not fear (Luke 8:22-25). And his constant message is: 'Do not be afraid for I shall be with you'. Jesus will be with us throughout the event, as he was with Stephen. '... God was with him and brought him safely through all his troubles' (Acts 7:9-10).

Christ and I are in this together! He isn't going to desert us at our hour of need. He, who longs to put his arms round all his people, '... just as a hen gathers her chicks under her wings' (Matthew 23:37). We can seek shelter in the arms of Christ. My goodness, the death of a Christian should indeed be filled with light and hope! '... you must live like people who belong to the light' (Ephesians 5:8), so surely we must also die like people who belong to the light.

'Be joyful always, pray at all times, be thankful in all circumstances' (1 Thessalonians 5:16). Thankful even when dying. Or *especially* when dying!

God is with us. 'O send forth your light and your truth; let these be my guide. Let them bring me to your holy mountain to the place where you dwell' (Psalm 42:3).

Yes, death is the great giving up – but in order to have something which is so much better – life after death.

'Christ died for our sins... he was raised to life three days later' (1 Corinthians 15:3,4). If Christ had not been raised to life, then our faith would be delusion, but we believe those who were witnesses to his Resurrection.

'If our hope in Christ is good for this life only and no more, then we deserve more pity than anyone else in all the world. But the truth is that Christ has been raised from death, as the guarantee that those who sleep in death will also be raised ... all will be raised to life because of their union with Christ' (1 Corinthians 15:19-22). If we believe in Christ's Resurrection, then we have no reason to doubt in our own.

'We know that God, who raised the Lord Jesus to life, will also raise us up with Jesus and take us ... into his presence' (2 Corinthians 4:14). *Know. Trust.* And help others to believe through the hope we have at our death. 'We must wear faith and love as a breastplate, and our hope of salvation as a helmet' (1 Thessalonians 5:8). A very elaborate regalia for the finale! Personally, I'd love to also have joy, as expressed by Thomas More in what is reputed to be his last prayer – 'Pray for me as I pray for you and for all our friends: that we may love and laugh again when we meet merrily in heaven!'

'... you belong to Christ, and Christ belongs to God' (1 Corinthians 3:23). Of course we will be saved!

And so we come to the passage between earth and heaven – the birth canal to everlasting life. Our final experience of being born again!

The grain of wheat drops into the ground and dies when the corn is ripe!

The passage to heaven
The light at the end of the tunnel – is this the image of dying that most of us carry? Will that tunnel be dark? Or long? Or rough? Or will we slip through, lubricated by the love of those who pray for us? All other gifts and qualities we must lay aside at death, but love goes with us.

Is it a tunnel through which we walk? Or are we pushed? Our birth journey through the vagina can affect the whole quality of our lives, as does the development within the womb. Are there analogies to be made with our emergence into heaven? Could eternal life be coloured by the quality of our preparation for death, and the ease of our transition?

Will a life devoted to getting to know Christ ease us quickly along the passage? Or will we be flushed along by the Spirit?

Do we slip and slide through the tunnel, emerging head first to the vision of heaven? Or will it be like walking on water?

Does each person have their own unique experience of this journey, appropriate to both their temperament and their interests? The adventurous, the curious, the traveller, the scientist, the timid, the lover, the poet, the musician, etc.

Are we learning and changing all the way?

Will we have the sensation of being squeezed along? Or will we be left free and tumbling in space like many a dream?

Are we born into heaven explosively? Or borne – as in carried?

Will the Holy Spirit accompany us? Or will we follow Christ through the tunnel? Or will he walk beside us all the way, explaining the scriptures and God's promise to us, as on that walk to Emmaus?

Will we recognise him only at the journey's end?

The meeting

Whatever our experience is, whatever the barrier is, once through, we will certainly see and know Christ in all his glory. '... remain in union with him, so that when he appears we may be full of courage and need not hide in shame from him on the Day he comes' (1 John 2:28).

'The people who live in darkness

will see a great light.

On those who live in the dark land of death

the light will shine' (Matthew 4:16, quoting Isaiah 9:1&2).

Yes, from where we stand on earth, death can seem like darkness. But we Christians know that the Light shines in all darkness, and we know that Light is Christ.

'"I am the light of the world", he said. "Whoever follows me will have the light of life and will *never* walk in dark-ness"' (John 8:12; emphasis mine). So Christ's light must even illuminate that tunnel!

115

Death, it would seem, is not so much a finale as a brilliant beginning. A triumph, not a tragedy. The great and wonderful meeting of friends.

'God was making all mankind his friends through Christ' (1 Corinthians 5:19). Either we know him and are already in love with him, or we will fall instantly in love on meeting.

We will see him, transformed and beautiful as Matthew described him in the Transfiguration (Matthew 17:1-8). This too is how we will become!

'...we know that when Christ appears, we shall be like him, because we shall see him as he really is' (l John 3:2).

His glory will shine on us and transform us. We will know that our light is his reflected light.

'Your real life is Christ and when he appears, then you too will appear with him and share his glory' (Colossians 3:4).

How can we doubt this repeating message? How can we fail to be excited? Awed? Aghast? Agape?

But, 'he will be gentle to those who are weak, and kind to those who are helpless' (Matthew 12:20). And won't we all arrive both weak and helpless?

Maybe this is the reason why God allows old age or ill-health or accident to weaken our mortal bodies, so that we are helpless before the Lord and thus made ready to receive his glory.

He not only strengthens us, but he also purifies us. 'He will also keep you firm to the end, so that you may be faultless on the Day of our Lord Jesus Christ' (l Corinthians 1:8).

The day of our Lord Jesus Christ!

The crescendo of our lives! And if we have implicitly trusted in his love, we will be faultless. He will have forgotten our sins! It is enough to send us off into peals of incredulous and hysterical laughter!

The final paragraph of G.K. Chesterton's *Orthodoxy* speaks thus of Jesus:

There was something that he hid from all men when he went up a mountain to pray. There was something that he covered constantly by abrupt silence or impetuous isolation. There was some one thing that was too great for God to show us when he walked upon our earth; and I have sometimes fancied that it was his mirth.

Won't that be lovely, if the Lord is laughing too!

Purgatory
When he was on earth, Jesus never frightened sinners. Rather, he attracted them.

When we meet him, we will not be afraid of him either. We will love him with an instant intensity that is beyond our present capacity. But his light will also be the light of knowledge and understanding.

That light of understanding will lead us to total self-realisation. And this must surely be our purgatory. We will clearly see our hypocrisy, our greed, our lust, our manipulations, our self-centredness. All will be illuminated.

'The Lord turned round and looked straight at Peter' (Luke 22:61), and this will be our agony too; the Lord looking straight at us, seeing all, as we realise what we have done against him! Or what we have not done for him!

'Peter went out and wept bitterly' (Luke 22:62), and we too will have bitter tears to shed. We will suddenly know exactly how much the Lord has loved and longed for us, as well as how much he has had to forgive us. What agony that debt will be to us. We will have no excuse to justify our sins. Jesus will offer no excuses for his enveloping love.

Not only will we know Jesus and ourselves, but also all those we have ever known. We will see how they could have been, if we had loved and cared for them more.

The only thing we will have of value as we stand before our loving Lord, is how much we have loved selflessly and how we have accepted the love of others.

117

All the rest is so much dross in our lives. It will fall away, leaving only that which was based in Christ's love. Imagine, then, our smallness!

Maybe the missed opportunities will cause our greatest remorse. 'Why didn't I invest all my energies in serving him?' will be our aching lament.

Yes, surely this Last Judgment will be self-judgment, plus perhaps the judgment of those who have not yet forgiven us.

We have to be purged of all this. We have to be changed before we can be brought before the Almighty. Releasing ourselves, gratefully, to be changed in the Lord's hands, will be our first perfect prayer.

We will have to let go of our bigotry, our narrowness, our disgust. We will have to make good our lack of love and understanding until we see with Christ's eyes and feel with his heart. For certain, Jesus will have creative ways of changing us!

Maybe we will meet selected people. Jesus might introduce the fundamentalist to the Queen of Heaven – his mother. Mary might introduce the Catholic to her son – James! He could point out the instigator of our redemption – Judas. The white king will see the black man rule, and so on through the ranks of the unexpected.

We will catch glimpses of chief rabbis and old popes playing together with little children, and learning from them. We might be left in the care of a loving group of people, until it dawns on us who they are: the doctor we blamed for our husband's death; the teacher we hated; the brother we have never forgiven; the priest we couldn't stand and the vandals down the road.

There is a lot to change! Will we grow gradually through this change, so growing into heaven?

When Jesus was asked to describe the kingdom of heaven (Luke 13:18-19), he spoke of a mustard seed growing huge, and of yeast rising. Was he suggesting that from our infinitesimal smallness and insignificance, we will grow to greatness in heaven?

Do we gradually become one with the glorified Body of Christ as the Father answers the pleas of his Son and the prayers of our relatives and friends?

Or is it much more instant?

'I promise you', Jesus said to the good thief, 'that *today* you will be in Paradise with me' (Luke 23:43; emphasis mine). The whole changing process done as quickly as a butterfly emerging from the chrysalis!

'... we shall all be changed in an instant, as quickly as the blinking of an eye' (1 Corinthians 15:52). The agony of purgatory is pretty quick then? So much work done on us in that moment!

'... the time comes for all things to be made new' (Acts 3:21). Think of all the aches and pains we carry. All the blemishes and defects. All the mis-shapes and mishaps – all put right! Alleluia! No wonder we don't look the same!

Maybe the very defects we suffered will become the most beautiful parts. My bunions will gleam with glory!

'When (the body is) buried, it is ugly and weak; when raised, it will be beautiful and strong' (1 Corinthians 15:43). This is how our loved ones will be also – different but recognisable in their glory.

In the way that we know that a tulip bulb will change into a tulip flower; a red admiral caterpillar will become a red admiral butterfly; a small blue egg will become a blackbird; so we will know each changed friend. They will be totally but connectably different and therefore recognisable.

('Cognition' – 'knowing, in the widest sense, including sensation, perception, etc.' *Chamber's English Dictionary*)

What breathtaking recognitions will take place!

'When you sow a seed in the ground, it does not sprout to life unless it dies. And what you sow is a bare seed ... not the full-bodied plant that will later grow up' (1 Corinthians 15:36-37). Where is the sorrow in letting the seed die if we are to become full-bodied and beautiful plants? What a prospect!

119

Life is full of clues about how God likes to transform things. We are told of Jesus' transfiguration, but we too sometimes experience simple things in our own lives that transform us momentarily and, as we say, lift us 'out of this world'.

We do not initiate these occasions. They are pure gift from God. A glimpse of heaven. The scales falling temporarily from our eyes. 'The veil is removed only when a person is joined to Christ' (2 Corinthians 3:14).

Through our union with Christ in heaven we will be permanently transformed. 'While he was praying, his face changed its appearance' (Luke 9:29). This will happen to us too as we are changed in heart and understanding. Our whole bodies will become transfigured, as will all we have suffered. 'If the Spirit of God ... lives in you, then he who raised Christ from death will also give life to your mortal bodies by the presence of his Spirit in you' (Romans 8:11).

'It is through Christ that all of us are able to come in the one Spirit into the presence of the Father' (Ephesians 2:18). '... thanks be to God who gives us the victory through our Lord Jesus Christ!' (1 Corinthians 15:57).

'... before the world was made, God had already chosen us to be his through our union with Christ, so that we would be holy and without fault before him' (Ephesians 1:4).

The whole blessed Trinity is working for us, to heal us and to bring us to perfection! Because of this, and because of Christ's redemptive act of love, we will stand before God, holy and faultless. Nothing of this do we deserve. We are unworthy and unholy, but Jesus has taken away our guilt and given us his glory. That is how the Almighty Father wants to meet us. Who are we to argue!

What we must do in this life is to minimise the infliction of our sins upon the Lord. Our greatest sin would be to ignore his gifts and fail to believe his promises.

We must believe and accept – like children – *today*.

Heaven

When we claim our inheritance – what will it be like? The Book of Revelation gives me goose pimples! So many people standing around in long white robes! *For ever?* They *are* praising God, but that kind of praise seems impossibly dull to me.

If I could concentrate on God for all eternity, I'd want to do more active praising than just standing! I'd want to dance and leap and sing and paint! But there's the rub! That would be what *I* would be wanting to do, and the *I* will have become submerged into the God.

Nevertheless, the monotony (dare I ever use that word in association with adoration of God? No, I daren't really, but it *is* part of my present human reaction!), the sameness of standing still for ever and ever and ever ... appals me. It surely can't possibly be like that.

Or do I totally misapprehend? Too limited in love and homage? Too full of self-gratification even in my loving God? God help me!

But Lord – standing for ever! I might as well be a tree!

No, I imagine heaven as being incredibly full of variety; full of light and subtle, changing colours as in a beautiful sunset sky; of music, harmonies and music-making; of love and laughter and delight in each other's company, with the Lord ever present, ever in mind, ever central to all.

We will play like children before our parents, conscious that we give joy to the Almighty. We will know how we are loved by God and that will make all things good.

If we have work to do, that will give us pleasure and satisfaction. There will be no disharmony, no rivalry, no inadequacy, no injustice, but surely there will be plenty to do.

Everyone will have their own place and function within the whole Body of Christ. Each part working for the good of the whole. (I suppose, then, some could be standing still some of the time. Perhaps some might even *choose* to stand still in silent adoration! Even I might want to stand still occasionally!)

There will be lots of surprises and personal intimacies with God. 'To those who win the victory I will give some of the hidden manna. I will also give each of them a white stone on which is written a new name that no one knows except the one who receives it' (Revelation 2:17).

Just think what the possible new name might be: faithful one; lovely one; my delight; joyous one; gentle heart; delicate soul; ... or what? The name will be written like a secret love letter. It will convey the essence of what God enjoys in us. It will be exceedingly special and precious. We will savour it and rejoice in it and know that it is uniquely right. Alleluia! We will be gleefully conscious of God's personal love for us.

'He who sits on the throne will protect them with his presence. Never again will they hunger or thirst; neither sun nor any scorching heat will burn them, because the Lamb, who is in the centre of the throne, will be their shepherd, and he will guide them to springs of life-giving water. And God will wipe away every tear from their eyes' (Revelation 7:15-17). Eternal life will be rich, abundant and exquisite and we shall enjoy it with childlike wonder and enthusiasm, always mindful of God.

'Let the children come to me, and do not stop them, because the Kingdom of God belongs to such as these. I assure you that whoever does not receive the Kingdom of God like a child will never enter it' (Mark 10:14-15).

We are to be childlike – wide-eyed; eager; expectant; full of joyful anticipation; accepting; trusting; willing; cooperative; able to give and receive gifts of love; owning nothing; acknowledging our total dependence upon God. (We used to have a dog that was better qualified than I am!)

For us, to know the Father will be to love him.

Eternal life, then, will be a living love.

Loving for ever.

Loving all those who also love God.

Our one common denominator will be the love of God.

If we like the idea of true love – *agape* – then heaven is for us. Our loving will give glory to God. God's love will give glory to us. If we like the idea of glory, then heaven is for us. If we think we are well blessed now – just wait and see, because 'the person who has something will be given more ...' (Mark 4:25).

We have no reason to doubt that our experience after death will be infinitely richer than our life on earth.

'What we see now is like a dim image in a mirror; then we shall see face to face. What I know now is only partial; then it will be complete – as complete as God's knowledge of me' (1 Corinthians 13:12). Heaven will be knowledge and understanding as well as being known and understood. How much earthly frustration occurs because we feel we are not completely understood, even within our closest relationships.

But God will '... set our whole being free' (Romans 8:23). Freedom from all misunderstandings. Freedom from restrictions. Freedom of movement, of feeling, of spirit. Freedom to be utterly ourselves. Freedom to love extravagantly, like the Lord does.

Heaven will be fantastic – God is so ridiculously generous. It is bound to be much better than the very best on earth, and far better than the most outrageous imaginings.

God will give us a new body, personally fashioned for us. It will have suffered no damage or distortion. It will be perfect and a free gift from God because he loves us and we love him.

We can be sure that our spiritual bodies will somehow contain the best of our individuality. We will lose nothing good from our personalities. Our new bodies will be rooted in the old. Our joy and happiness will be limitless because of the perfection and tenderness of heavenly love.

This is what death leads to! No wonder Paul was in a hurry to get there. But I believe that first we are meant to enjoy as many earthly experiences as possible and to be the means of helping others to do the same, in appreciation of God's gift of life and his many other blessings.

Will people enjoy heaven to different degrees in the same way as people have varying capacities to enjoy life on earth? Whatever our different capacities, we will be content. There are many mansions in heaven. Maybe we will not be offered a palace, but in succumbing to the love of God, we will be happy in a shed and see it as perfect for us.

> 'How lovely is your dwelling place,
> Lord, God of hosts' (Psalm 83:2).

All will delight us and our delight will give God praise – as it can do here on earth.

Those we have loved on earth are sure to be there with us, as heaven would be less than perfect without them. Our very loving of them ensures their presence. (So we do well to love widely here on earth!) But God is the source of all love. He wouldn't have created any of us if we didn't enhance his pleasure in some way.

The energy level of loving must be incredible!

So heaven seems to be all about love and growth and beauty and joy and much, much more that we are unable to envisage. It has little to do with sleeping or resting in peace, or even standing. We even feast with the Lord:

'You will eat and drink at my table in my Kingdom' (Luke 22:30). The whole of heaven, and all who are there, will be shining with the glory of God. Every moment will be a celebration of our resurrection. We won't have an instant of indifference to Christ's redeeming act, ever again. God will draw forth the beauty of our uniqueness in perfect praise.

> How great is our God!
> How deep are his designs!
> Honour and glory to him for ever and ever!
> Why do we fail to believe his promises?

Why don't we look to death with excitement and anticipation? I am certainly beginning to! No, far from being frightened by contemplating heaven, it has given me strong motivation to get there!

Meeting the Almighty

'Everyone must die once, and after that be judged by God' (Hebrews 9:27). 'Honour God and praise his greatness! For the time has come for him to judge mankind' (Revelation 14:7).

There is here the suggestion that we will be judged both individually and as a group. There is also the clear statement that we will *all* have to go into the presence of Almighty God. Then it is that we need the support of Christ as never before.

'In union with Christ and through our faith in him we have the boldness to go into God's presence with all confidence' (Ephesians 3:12). We would be better off without our human bodies at this stage, because the thumping hearts would be deafening! But – he will be pleased to see us! Isn't that difficult to believe, but believe it we *must*!

'Let us have confidence, then, and approach God's throne, where there is grace. There we will receive mercy and find grace to help us just when we need it' (Hebrews 4:16).

'We have ... complete freedom to go into the Most Holy Place by means of the death of Jesus. He opened for us a new way, a living way, through the curtain – that is, through his own body' (Hebrews 10:19). This is the curtain we pass through at death. Jesus has paid the high price of our entry ticket.

Although Jesus was speaking to the Apostles about coming before earthly rulers when he said 'Make up your minds beforehand not to worry about how you will defend yourselves, because I will give you such words and wisdom that none of your enemies will be able to refute or contradict what you say' (Luke 21:14-15), we can equally rely on Jesus to give us the means to face our heavenly Judge. We cannot defend ourselves. He can and will. It is not we who make this happen, but God.

We will stand before the Almighty: 'Every one of us, then, will have to give an account of himself to God' (Romans 14:12), by which time, we will know ourselves in all the intimate details of our weakness.

Standing in this place, we can have confidence only in Jesus. We will already have been made holy and purified by courtesy of Christ. He will plead for us, as will the Holy Spirit: '... the Spirit pleads with God on behalf of his people' (Romans 8:27). 'And the quality of each person's work will be seen when the Day of Christ exposes it!' (1 Corinthians 3:13).

If that prospect causes us embarrassment, as it is likely to do, remember the dirty pieces of handiwork that our children brought home from school. How welcome and honoured they were when they represented their best efforts – because we loved them. God loves us.

'God knows us completely' (2 Corinthians 5:11), and still he loves us. He will love us no less when we stand before him to be judged. Our sins will be no shock to him – only to us! Indeed, he seems remarkably uninterested in sin: 'I will not remember their sins and evil deeds any longer' (Hebrews 10:17). A deliberate forgetting! A fresh start, yet formed on the past. For the Almighty is just: 'I will repay each one of you according to what he has done' (Revelation 2:23).

And God's judgment will be infinitely accurate. So although we are loved, understood and forgiven all, we also get our just desserts, whatever that may entail.

We will know the judgment to be utterly right. We will be satisfied. A thimble can be full to its brim the same as a bucket. But however unworthy we are, God longs to gift us as he has promised. 'Because of his love God had already decided that through Jesus Christ he would make us his sons (and daughters) – this was his pleasure and purpose' (Ephesians 1:4-5).

Think of our own delight as we await the homecoming of one of our children for whom we have a special present. What pleasure we get from anticipating their joy. That must be how God waits for us! And his gift? – we inherit the Kingdom of Heaven! Why me? Because that is why God made me! What a God! Why need we fear meeting him?

'He gave us his Son – will he not also freely give us all things?'(Romans 8:32). Alleluia! Alleluia!

What ecstasy if he says: 'Well done, you good and faithful servant.... Come on in and share my happiness' (Matthew 25:21).

Even those of us who have dishonoured him will receive his gifts according to his promises, because God gives in the way he chooses, like the man who hired workers for his vineyard, and no one can argue with that (Matthew 20:1-16). We Christians might be compared to those who grafted away all day in the heat of the sun, to be given the same as the atheist who meets Jesus on the point of death, and loves him.

We can't complain. We can rejoice for the atheist, 'Or are you jealous because I am generous?' (Matthew 20:15).

'So those who are last will be first, and those who are first will be last' (Matthew 20:16). We may have striven all our lives to be good servants of God, simply so that others might have a greater share of God's glory! How I would rejoice if this were for my children. And when I am purified by Christ, I will rejoice for any of God's people, even my former enemies. What jealousies we have to eliminate in that time of purge and change! Maybe this is what being Christian is all about.

'See how much the Father has loved us! His love is so great that we are called God's children – and so in fact we are ... we are now God's children, but it is not yet clear what we shall become' (1 John 3:1-2).

127

Our knowledge of God leads us to be optimistic! Excited! Confident! God can be trusted. This trust can be learned and experienced over a lifetime of union with Christ. It is unrealistic to expect suddenly to experience it after a lifetime of indifference to God – and yet – God has his ways and means to bring about the impossible (not to mention the prayers of others, especially mothers!). The timing too is his choice, as he well illustrated in the parable about hiring the labourers. He gives to the indifferent as generously as to the ardent.

How the previously indifferent must love him when they come face to face with such breathtaking generosity!

10

BEREAVEMENT

'O precious in the eyes of the Lord
is the death of his faithful' (Psalm 115:15).

So death is the climax of a Christian's life. The crescendo! All the glory that we have just imagined, and far, far more, is being experienced by our beloved dead.

Time is not an element of heaven. Once through the barrier of death, all is in the present. The dead, through Jesus Christ, our Lord, are in ecstasy. They are perfected.

We can imagine their meeting with Christ. He will see in them all that we loved them for and much, much more besides. He is loving them better than we ever could. They are whole and content. But what about those who are left behind?

Bereavement is not always a painful experience. Sometimes death can be a great release for all concerned. The peaceful death of an elderly person carries no regrets. But when the death is of someone whom we love intensely – the one in whom we have invested so much of our happiness — the loss can be agonising, at a time when we may be physically and emotionally exhausted from intensive caring or shock.

No one truly envisages this loss until it has become their own personal experience. It is pain of the heart and the mind, and very often a physical pain too. We become wounded people, vulnerable to so many other unsuspected hurts and difficulties. Chasms of despair can open up before us, suddenly and without any warning. We, who were competent and balanced people can teeter on the brink, stunned by our own inadequacy.

Shock; numbness; realisation of the enormity of our loss; denial; anger; fear; a sense of inadequacy; panic; blame; remorse; guilt; lack of motivation; emptiness; relief; loneliness – are some of the contradictory and often unreasonable emotions that form the turmoil within us.

Bereavement is like an amputation of half of ourselves, or even a double death, as a friend of mine expressed it: 'My husband is dead, and I am no longer a wife!'

Our role of wife, or husband, or parent or friend, is suddenly cancelled out. It is as if we do not know what part to play in life. We feel redundant. The whole personality is assaulted by the death of someone emotionally close. Such grief is overwhelming! It absorbs our whole attention.

When the shock wears off, we suffer acutely. As time goes by, slowly, we begin to adapt, as we do to any other handicap. The pain becomes a dull, but chronic ache that we get used to. The whole balance and order of our lives is altered. We have to learn a whole new ball game – alone and disabled.

Bereavement through sudden death has special problems, because the shock compounds the difficulties. It does such violence to the normality of our lives. We are deprived of the opportunity to do the caring described earlier. To those suddenly bereaved, all those opportunities to serve and share seem incredibly joyful and privileged work. Maybe we wouldn't have done it that way, or we might have done it better – but we never had the chance to try.

No time to work on grief together. So much unsaid; unsorted; unprepared. All the guilts, the longings and 'if onlys'. No time to say 'Goodbye – I love you.' Life left half done – or so it seems to us.

Not so to God. It is his choice of time. Their work for him is complete.

For us, there is no right time to part with those we love. I have shared the agony of one who over three years watched her intelligent husband slowly deteriorate to a non-person.

She sees sudden death as a great blessing. But I cannot console her with the pain of another friend who never said 'Goodbye'.

The truth is, they are blessed who are called quickly to the Lord and meet him as a friend. 'How happy are those servants whose master finds them awake and ready when he returns! I tell you, he will take off his coat, ask them to sit down, and will wait on them' (Luke 12:37).

Stay with that image, those who have suddenly lost loved ones. In imagination, watch your loved one being served this way by Christ. And be at peace.

If the sudden death is caused by another's carelessness, or, worse still, a deliberate act of violence – the bereaved can experience a turmoil of overwhelming feelings of anger, hatred and revenge. The death seems *not* to be God's choice of time, but the choice of someone else, who has no right to choose.

These fierce emotions lie dormant in us all. To have them suddenly unleashed and sent rampaging through our whole being is terrifying in itself. We can suspect madness. We desperately need help, but often it is our chosen helper who has been deliberately or carelessly taken from us.

My God! How we need your help in the chaos of our minds and hearts. And we need the help of all who can give us understanding support. We are not rational people at this time.

But God can take the very worst of happenings (even a wrongful crucifixion of the Son of God) and use them for the good of all who love him. The trouble is, from our human perspective, we have to take that fact on trust.

'Calm your anger and forget your rage;
do not fret, it only leads to evil' (Psalm 36:8). We need the help of all the praying community to be able to do that.

'Christ gave his life for us. We too, then, ought to give our lives for our brothers!' (1 John 3:16).

And there are those who, within some tragic circumstances, are given this opportunity – and take it. Maybe our loved ones have had this privilege.

For those who fear that their loved ones have in fact turned their backs on the Lord – don't underestimate the Almighty: '... because of God's choice, they are his friends ... For God does not change his mind about whom he chooses and blesses' (Romans 11:28-29). He will have called them at a moment when they could return to him, maybe through the very evil that they encountered in the final moments of their lives.

And '... if the roots of a tree are offered to God, the branches are his also' (Romans 11:16). How deeply we must root ourselves in the Lord through all the agony of loss. It is a time of great testing, as is all bereavement.

'... the seed is the Word of God ... But it does not sink deep into them; ... when the time of testing comes, they fall away' (Luke 8:11-13). The Word of God must become part of our very being long before the time of bereavement. Then we will have trust in Christ, whatever circumstances surround the death.

To be Christian is to believe in Christ, his Resurrection, and the redemption and resurrection of all our loved ones. No death, however violent or obscene, can cancel out God's promise. Cling on to this throughout the darkest times.

No Christian who believes in the Resurrection can be sorry for the one who is dead. All pain is over for them. God has already perfected their happiness. The loss which over-whelms us is all ours, not theirs. They are enriched beyond all our imaginings. We have to let them go to God and rejoice for them, however broken-hearted we are without them. '... we want you to know the truth about those who have died, so that you will not be sad, as are those who have no hope. We believe that Jesus died and rose again, and so we believe that God will take back with Jesus those who have died believing in him.'

Yet we do mourn, and because we are human, we need to

132

mourn, as Mary did, when she stood crying beside the Lord's tomb. If our loved ones could speak to us, they would say, much as the Risen Christ said to her, 'I am returning to him who is my Father and your Father, my God and (your) God' (John 20:17).

Our loved ones must return to God. We, who are left, are left for a reason. Part of God's plan. He hasn't got it the wrong way round. We are not living out some dreadful mistake – though it can most certainly feel like that at times. Trust God, and the very way we behave will teach others about our belief in the Lord's mercy and his promise of eternal life.

Jesus himself understood every one of our raw emotions. His Passion contains all, from his shattering fear to his disbelief that all this was really happening to him. I imagine that throughout his agony on the cross, he felt that his Father would rescue him at some point and show his glory to the world. That his Father didn't do this, caused his cry of despair at feeling utterly forsaken.

No, none of our emotions is new to Jesus. He is with us, sharing every agony. He does not abandon us at any stage of our grief, not even if we turn our fury and condemnation on him. He understands the chaos within and will hold us tight until the storm is over, as a mother holds a child that is frightened by its rage. 'The Lord is close to the broken-hearted' (Psalm 33:19).

Try not to be afraid. Rely on God's strength in our weakness. We can unite our agony to Christ's and hope it too will be transformed to give glory to God.

Jesus' mother was warned by Simeon: '...sorrow, like a sharp sword, will break your own heart' (Luke 2:35). Even she was not spared grief. Bereavement would seem to be a necessary part of God's plan for the redemption of the world. We may not understand. We are asked to accept it and allow God's will to be done, trusting him as Mary did. 'God's will be done, not mine' – our constant prayer.

Bereavement has to be different for a Christian. There is such great purpose in death – there must be equal purpose in suffering grief. God, if offered it, will use it. Through it he can teach us to transfer our focus from self to him and on to others.

It is a daily taking up of the cross – just to get up and face the lonely ache of another day. Our crosses can be carried willingly or resentfully. But 'Whoever does not carry his own cross and come after me cannot be my disciple' (Luke 14:27).

Around illness, death and bereavement, there are many crosses to bear. Be glad – our loved ones are saved the pain we suffer.

'Happy are those who mourn;
God will comfort them!' (Matthew 5:4).

God moves close to us and we can become acutely aware of his presence. Seek his consolation. Read the Scriptures. Work with the Holy Spirit, searching for understanding and for a strengthening of faith. Read of God's promise for his children and know our loved ones are transformed. Rejoice for *them* even though our hearts are breaking.

Pray for them that they will be able to accept all that God offers them. Prayer brings us into God's presence – which is where our loved ones are. Feel close to them through Jesus.

Our prayers may even rant and rave against the Lord at times. We are not the first.

'How long must I bear grief in my soul,
this sorrow in my heart day and night?' (Psalm 12:3). His love will remain constant throughout, as we will discover.

Pray at all times – minimum prayers when we are confused and troubled, just calling on the name of Jesus – long, resting meditation when we are more composed. 'Be still and know that I am God' (Psalm 45:11).

There will be certain times of the day that are specially difficult. Try, then, to move close to God. A friend suffered intensely, just before going up to bed. He learnt to convert it into a time when he relaxed into Christ's care. He would then recall his wife's voice, touch, memory. From the worst time, it became the most precious part of the day. We can all be healed like this.

'A widow who is all alone, with no one to take care of her, has placed her hope in God and continues to pray and ask him for his help night and day' (1 Timothy 5:5). If we belong to a praying community, they too will pray with us for healing. We will be renewed.

Can bereavement, then, become a great prayer experience?

While we are grieving, we need to feel that we are still loved, understood and supported – therefore, accept all help to carry the cross – as Jesus did. Family and friends are invaluable at this time, particularly if they will allow us to go on talking freely of our loved ones, for as long as we have a need to.

It is important that we struggle to express our deep feelings. In voicing them, we release the pressure they build up within us. The difficulty often is that the very one we trusted with our deepest feelings is now gone.

Bereavement counselling can help. In talking over the turmoil, we bring order out of the chaos.

For those who support – tread carefully upon our suffering. Do not deny the feelings of the bereaved, however irrational they may seem. That makes them no less real – only more confusing. Stay beside us while we sort out the confusion for ourselves. Do not make decisions for us, even when we try hard to trap you into doing so. Do not be hurt by our anger or our over-sensitivity. Just try to understand our daily pain. We are vulnerable and emotionally unstable. We are lonely and frightened and pretending we are not. We can even suspect that we are going mad. Hold us tight. Pray for us and with us. Share your faith to reinforce ours. 'We who are strong in faith ought to help the weak to carry their burdens' (Romans 15:1).

God will heal us through your compassion and we will come to a point of acceptance.

Through our acceptance of grief, we learn patient endurance in submitting to the will of God. This is our major lesson in learning to die to self. It is very, very painful. So was Christ's death. Jesus, '... even though he was God's Son, ... learnt through his sufferings to be obedient' (Hebrews 5:8). As we must do.

If we are well-practised in learning to die, we will understand and accept bereavement. That doesn't remove the pain, but it can ease the panic and despair and it removes the sense of purposelessness. And certainly it is better to accept death with love rather than anger.

Gradually, we come to give all willingly to God – including our loved ones. They are not ours to possess. We have shared our lives with them for some length of time and for that we must give God praise and thanks, however short the time has been.

'My Father has given me all things' (Luke 10:22), and all we have had was God-given. We are not meant to cling for ever. '... none of you can be my disciple unless he gives up everything he has' (Luke 14:33).

We have been asked to give up our loved ones. Can we who grieve, help our dead departed by relinquishing our hold on them? We are so interdependent through the Body of Christ that one part affects another for good or otherwise. 'Do not hold on to me' (John 20:17), Jesus said to Mary in the garden.

Imagine, once again, the meetings of our loved ones with the Father and the Son. See them being loved and changed to perfection. Let go and give them back to the Creator, with thanks. Here indeed is the 'fine and beautiful thing' that we can give to Jesus.

Personally, the one I love led me to Christ's love. Maybe his death will bring me even closer to Christ. He will be happy about that.

There doesn't seem to be a short-cut to the process of grief. Perhaps there isn't meant to be. But we can be helped to move through the experience as smoothly as possible, to a point of acceptance, adjusting to a new way of life, with new motivations. 'May the Lord look on you with favour and bring you peace' (Numbers 6:27).

How right Freud was when he suggested that we understood things better after they were broken!

We are being changed!
Through bereavement, we are often forced into radical change. If we believe that God chooses the time of death, it is only logical to believe that the time for us to change is his choice too.

Christ is at work in us through all the traumas and exultations that we experience in life. He is changing us as we pray and when we do anything that draws us into his company. I have changed, since starting to puzzle over this subject of death. The Holy Spirit is working within any struggle to discern the will of God.

It is essential that we put our changing into God's hands. That way we will grow rather than diminish. '... the sadness that is used by God brings a change of heart that leads to salvation – and there is no regret in that!' (2 Corinthians 7:10). An important part of being Christian is allowing ourselves to be changed by God; accepting the changes and even seeking to be changed. He is preparing us for our meeting with himself.

There has been no more dramatic change for the good of the whole of humankind, than that brought about by Christ's death. Yet at the time, all his friends were utterly shattered. They mourned his loss and struggled with the bitterness of his failure.

The Risen Christ himself walked with them to Emmaus and through the Scriptures showed them that it hadn't been a ghastly mistake; he had had to suffer; the Crucifixion was necessary; it was all part of God's plan for humankind. '... he opened their minds to understand the Scriptures' (Luke 24:45).

We all have to make our own journey to Emmaus. If we walk with him, the Lord will teach us to understand the purpose of both his Passion and ours, in the light of God's plan.

'May the Lord lead you into a greater understanding of God's love and the endurance that is given by Christ' (2 Thessalonians 3:5).

We begin to identify with Christ, seeing for the first time, maybe, all the grief he suffered through his friends as well as his enemies: rejection; loneliness; misunderstanding; failure; fear and physical pain.

We grow to a fuller understanding of ourselves and begin to accept our own failures and limitations. We see that in the eyes of God, our worth is not determined by our successes. We come to accept our frailty and mortality. This way we begin to grow in wisdom.

The change that is paramount, is that we become like little children. '... unless you change and become like children, you will never enter the Kingdom of heaven' (Matthew 18:3).

Like children, we must believe that our loving Father will give us all we need, including consolation when we are suffering, and strength when we are weakening. This way we receive God's peace.

'May the Lord himself, who is our source of peace, give you peace at all times and in every way' (2 Thessalonians 3:16). A peace beyond the understanding of the world that is so afraid of death. A peace that will teach others about the hope we carry in our hearts.

Do not run away, but begin *now* to look at what God wants us to do with the rest of our lives.

The Lord is forever presenting himself to us to be accepted or rejected. To accept is to live the present moment with him while holding an awareness of our future resurrection.

Like children – against all odds, we will win through to be able to rejoice again. If we cooperate with God, we will not stay emotionally wounded. We will be able to love again. Not in the same way as before, but more in God's way – *agape*. We will look outwards to those in need, and move willingly to where the Lord wants us to be. We will learn the precious lesson – we need not be afraid, God is with us. Through this experience of death, we touch Christ – maybe for the first time ever. This touch is undoubtedly strengthening. To be aware of Christ's strength, and to accept it, is to be healed. To capitalise on it is to become what God wants us to be – active followers of Christ.

'May the Lord make your love for one another and for all people grow more and more. ... In this way he will strengthen you, and you will be perfect and holy in the presence of our God and Father when our Lord Jesus comes with all who belong to him' (1 Thessalonians 3:12-13).

This is the resurrection towards which we look. Daily we live with this hope in us. Loving and serving because Christ loves and serves us. Until we come to our own death – the most dramatic and beautiful change we will ever encounter.

No, I have not found death a morbid or gruesome subject, utterly the contrary! What's more, facing death has given me an increased vitality for the present moment! Alleluia! Alleluia!

'You, Lord, give perfect peace, to those who keep their purpose firm and put their trust in you. Trust in the Lord for ever; he will always protect us' (Isaiah 26:3-4).